Church and Cinema

A Way of Viewing Film

Church
and Cinema

A Way of Viewing Film

by

JAMES M. WALL
Editor, *The Christian Advocate*

WILLIAM B. EERDMANS PUBLISHING COMPANY
Grand Rapids, Michigan

Portions of the chapter "Clinical, Psychological, and Lyrical: Sex in Cinema" originally appeared in *Christian Advocate*, September 17, 1970. All the film reviews in Chapter 6 are reprinted from the *Christian Advocate*, issue dates as indicated following each review. Copyright ©1966, 1967, 1968, 1969, 1970, 1971 The Methodist Publishing House.

The chapter "Let the Mother Go: Blacks in American Films" is adapted from an article that originally appeared in *South Today*.

Picture Credits:

A Man for All Seasons, Columbia Pictures; Copyright © 1971, Columbia Pictures Industries. *Midnight Cowboy*, *In the Heat of the Night*, and *Persona*, courtesy of United Artists Corporation. *Diary of a Country Priest*, Audio Brandon. *Z*, Cinema 5 Ltd. *Myra Breckinridge* and *Patton*, courtesy of Twentieth Century-Fox. *Last Summer* and *This Man Must Die*, Allied Artists.

6-19-23

CONTENTS

PREFACE

The *Christian Advocate* was begun in 1826 as a magazine for religious people; since 1956 it has been a professional journal for ministers. In nearly a century and a half of existence, the *Advocate* has changed in many ways. Many long-time readers would surely agree that one of the most noticeable changes in recent years has been its interest in the motion picture, not as a sin, but as an important art form.

The shift has been gradual. As managing editor of the *Advocate* I wrote my first film review for it in 1964, a strong attack on Otto Preminger's *The Cardinal,* objecting to its distortion of the Roman Catholic Church and its phony, slick handling of the racial situation. As editor of the *Advocate,* the first film article I solicited from another writer was a review of *Elmer Gantry,* a picture strongly critical of certain excesses in Protestant evangelicalism. The justification for placing each review in the magazine was that it dealt with religious themes. The review of *Elmer Gantry* was followed by reviews of *Becket* and *A Man for All Seasons;* and so the reviewing of religiously oriented pictures in the magazine was established.

From that timid beginning in 1964 my own handling of film criticism has evolved from a strictly religious preoccupation to an acceptance of film as film. This development came at a time when the theological world was dominated by discussions of secularization. The transition from a purely religious concern for film to a broader concern for film as film was made possible, in part, by a theological climate in which the reality of God came to be sought within secular structures as well as within the conventional religious structures.

Several years of teaching and lecturing in schools of theology and pastors' schools and many one-night stands in local churches encouraged me to pursue my study of film. The churchgoers and church leaders I have talked to have confirmed my belief that film is important for all ages. At the same time I have had an ongoing opportunity to write film criticism for various religious and secular magazines and journals. The central need I have discovered is for some way of viewing film that permits the non-scholar to make sense of the growing complexity of cinema. It is to meet that need that this book has been written.

It is largely because of the complexity of cinema that film viewing often evokes the kinds of argument found in discussions of religion and politics. Everyone who views a film has an opinion about what he has just seen. But like the experiences of religion and politics, the film experience can be enhanced — and opinions about it changed — by increased knowledge of the subject.

The study of film can be a massive undertaking. This book is not meant as a primer in that study. There are other books available that provide detailed examination of the history of cinema, the language of film, or close study of particular directors and genres of film. What is intended here is the presentation of a methodology, a means of evaluating film. The methodology proposed and tested is designed to establish a structure, an overall framework within which film discussion can be conducted. Reference will be made throughout the book to individual films in order to clarify the methodology. In the final chapter I have included specific reviews to provide the reader with examples of the methodology at work. I make no claims of eternal validity for the methodology itself. It is designed for the viewer who has a more-than-casual interest in film, and it is particularly aimed at bringing the filmgoer who is oriented to printed literature to an awareness of film as film.

Although my vocation is editing a magazine, my avocation is viewing and reviewing films. Like any buff in any field, I am obsessed with film. If it is on celluloid, I will watch it; but my own presupposition is that the filmmaker is handling sacred material. Woe unto him if he disappoints me! I hope that this book will prove to be a stimulus both for those who have just begun to take film seriously and for those who have long wanted to find handles by which to take hold of this important medium.

—James M. Wall

Chapter 1

WHAT HAS JERUSALEM TO DO WITH HOLLYWOOD?

The Church and Cinema

For many years — and even today for a minority of American churchgoers — the words "church and cinema" have suggested "church vs. cinema." Familiar images personifying the hostility of the church to Hollywood are those of the irate pastor storming the box office to stop the showing of a "dirty movie," and of the more august Roman Catholic Legion of Decency condemning a picture and bringing an entire industry to its knees in fear.

The Legion began its work in 1933, when American bishops determined that their collective power could be used to influence Hollywood's product. Accounts vary,* but it is generally accepted that Cardinal Dougherty of Philadelphia set in motion the forces that brought the Legion into existence. It is said that a huge billboard advertising — often luridly — the latest motion picture stood

*The version given here is that recorded in Jack Vizzard's *See No Evil* (Simon and Schuster, 1970). Space will not permit detailed discussion of the birth of the Legion, but this is an important part of the history of the church's relationship to the film industry. In an interview I conducted with Mr. Geoffrey Shurlock, Mr. Vizzard's superior in the Motion Picture Code and Rating Office, Mr. Shurlock recalled that the offending billboard referred to in Vizzard's version of the story was actually in Cincinnati, and the prelate who was offended was an Archbishop McNicholas. Shurlock did attribute the Warner agony and the European trip to Cardinal Dougherty, however. Further research in this period is needed, but the important fact is that the Legion was created out of Roman Catholic unhappiness over what it considered to be offensive films. The Vizzard version is written in a popular style. For a somewhat official industry version, the reader should examine Raymond Moley's *The Hays Office* (Bobbs, Merrill, 1945).

across the street from the Cardinal's home. One day a particularly obnoxious picture opening at the local Warner Brothers theater was featured. (The production companies and theaters were combined in those days.) The Cardinal, incensed, issued a statement forbidding Roman Catholics to enter a Warner Brothers theater; then he promptly departed on a trip to Europe, leaving Harry Warner faced with a grave financial crisis.

Warner quickly conferred with other leading Catholics, and the Legion was born. For the next thirty-five years this agency issued a rating for every motion picture made in Hollywood. An "A" picture could be seen by Catholics, but a "C" (condemned) picture was forbidden as an occasion of temptation to sin. Filmmakers soon discovered that it was easier to comply with Catholic requests to trim and cut their products than it was to release a picture tagged with the dreaded "C," which could get almost no bookings.

There are countless stories of attempts by angry ministers to prevent the showing of a film at a local theater. This kind of individual crusading has not yet passed from the scene entirely. As recently as 1969, a United Methodist pastor in South Dakota became incensed by the showing of *Candy* in a local theater. Accompanied by the sheriff, he had the print confiscated and the theater closed.

But if acting as vigilante at the box office was ever really a viable approach to cinema for the church, there can be no doubt that it is no longer so. For a number of reasons, the power of the church to influence the motion picture industry has largely gone the way of most prewar religious dreams. If the church pretends that it still has that kind of power it will content itself with random potshots that have little or no effect on those at whom they are directed.

In the face of this, the majority of churchgoers and church leaders have taken the easy way out: a sort of *laissez-faire* tolerance of movies. They make no attempt to influence or to interact with the products of the film industry. Pastors assume that many of their parishioners attend movies more or less regularly, just as many of them go to ball games, fish, or watch television. Filmgoing is, on this view, just another leisure time activity, commanding no more interest on the part of the church than any other. To put it another way, Jerusalem has nothing to do with Hollywood.

There is an alternative way that the church can confront this medium, an approach that reckons seriously with the power and influence of cinema in today's society. This approach is film education, conducted within the framework of the local church or any other group where concerned persons gather to examine and evaluate contemporary culture.

The suggestion that the church should educate its members to films raises two immediate questions: why should churchgoers be educated to film and why should the church do this educating?

The importance of cinema for the chuchgoer lies first of all in the revelational potential of the medium. The filmmaker is an artist who presents a vision of reality in his work, a vision that can enrich our own, *whether or not we share it*. And the churchgoer needs to be alerted and attuned to this source of revelation. We shall be elaborating on and illustrating this thesis throughout this book.

It is perhaps easier to see the importance of film when we consider it as a social phenomenon. At this level the tremendous potency of the medium is obvious. If we are to appreciate the power of film in contemporary life, it is crucial for us to evaluate its impact on society and recognize the influence it exercises in changing the values and moral standards of the community. In the process of making this evaluation it is imperative that we accept the film as a cinematic art form — albeit within a commercial mass market — in order that we might properly place our questions to the medium as a social phenomenon. Again, the need for film education is evident. The judgments and evaluations we make about a motion picture and about its impact on society must be informed judgments.

It is highly relevant, for example, to look at how American cinema has treated black people as characters or personalities over the last fifty years. This treatment has social implications, because it represents a clear example of American white racism. But we will be in a better position to make a judgment on this specific manifestation of racism if we do so with a clear understanding of the medium under consideration. In other words, an examination of the history of blacks in American films must be carried out within the context of *how* the subject is handled in this particular medium — the substance of the material itself — not with whether this topic is dealt with at all.

There was a time when what the church said about a particular social phenomenon made an enormous impact on the decisions of elected officials and community leaders just because the church said it. But that time is no more. The film industry today will listen to what the church says about film only if those who speak for the church display a knowledge of the medium they are criticizing and are not simply criticizing it because of surface reasons growing out of their own prior notions of ethics or morality.

The principle that judgment rendered on a secular matter from a theological perspective is effective only if it is at the same time well informed on the subject at hand is well illustrated in other areas where this principle is at work. For example, the most persuasive critics of American policy in Indochina are those churchmen who demonstrate that they are fully aware of the history of the area, of the various peace efforts that have been made, and of the military and political consequences of the various available foreign policy options. To point to another example, medical men are interested in ethical guidance in such emerging and complex areas as abortion, euthanasia, birth control, and organ transplants. They will not, however, respond to simplistic moralistic statements that reflect no awareness of the options available to the doctors and the complications involved in making such determinations as what is the exact moment that a fetus becomes a living organism or that a person actually dies.

Someone may object that, despite the power of film, it is still a matter that one can take or leave as he chooses, that film exercises an influence only on those who attend movies. We must be well aware that a cultural medium with the potency that film has exercises an impact far beyond the immediate viewing. From superficial things such as clothing styles to profound social attitudes, film affects the public. Clark Gable did not wear an undershirt in *It Happened One Night,* and the clothing industry noticed a distinct drop in sales of that item. The image of the black man in American films was not only influenced by the pattern of American racism that is causing the nation so much grief today, but it also helped to establish that pattern. World War II films inspired patriotism; the war films of the 1970s reflect the younger audience's disdain for war and also serve to reassure the young that their feeling about war is correct. And the nonfilmgoing public experiences these changes without ever visiting a theater.

Beyond concern for film as a cultural medium, we have suggested, is the matter of film as an art form, able to perform the renewing functions that have always been the task of art in our society. To a large extent, it is the young who accept film as art — their art — because it is the only art form unique to this technological century. The idea of a moving image did not become reality until technological advances late in the nineteenth century made it possible to project a picture in front of a light, hold it there for one-twenty-fourth of a second, and then move on to the next picture, thus creating the illusion of movement. There are still many older people who see films as escape and entertainment, but for the young — as well as for a surprising number of older viewers — film is an art form with its own history, culture, and language. These persons study the works of D. W. Griffith and Eric Von Stroheim with the same care that students of American literature give the writings of Hawthorne and Melville.

As an art form, film cannot be accepted casually. It has power that can be received either superficially or profoundly. Just as a Beethoven symphony may be no more than so much racket to the untrained ear, a work of film art may be "just another story" to the untrained eye. If film art is to provide the revitalizing experiences of which it is capable, film education is essential.

Such education will begin with the realization that film is both a cultural force and an art form, and that these two aspects can never be completely divorced. No art form is ever entirely without involvement with the culture from which it springs. Film's involvement with contemporary culture can often take the form of yielding to the temptation of commercialism, something to which the film is more vulnerable than, say, a painting. Unlike the painting, the film is sold many times. And it would be safe to say that most films produced over the last five decades have succumbed to this temptation: they have been formula works, lacking sensitivity and artistic significance. The fact of their production makes them culturally significant, however, for they reveal the interests and preoccupations of a people at a particular period of time. The racism and gangster interest of the 1930s, the flight from reality of the 1950s, the emphasis on sex, drugs, and student rebellion in the 1970s — all provide a clear indication for the student of social history of public concern for these subjects.

As an art form film must be judged severely. Many pictures can be dismissed as shallow, possessing little significance except as variations on particular themes and genres or lesser works of stars and directors. The kind of film education we are suggesting will enable viewers better to distinguish between films of little artistic significance and those of great importance. Furthermore, it will provide "handles of evaluation" through the use of which films of merit can work their magic on the viewer. A first viewing of Robert Bresson's *Diary of a Country Priest,* for example, may seem boring to the untrained eye. There is little action, and the overall pattern established by Bresson is grey and sad. But a closer study of the work of Bresson will begin to reveal certain themes in his films and particular techniques he uses to evoke certain moods and feelings. A second and third showing of *Diary of a Country Priest* will permit the film educator to lead the audience into richer experiences that have genuine meaning.

Film artists are part of our cultural heritage. We do not have to accept any of them. But we are the poorer if we do not have at least enough understanding of their importance to make a valid judgment about their merit. D. W. Griffith was always a little uneasy about his work as a film director. He had started on the stage and felt that the "movies" were a second-rate enterprise to which he would give only a little time until he was able to return to the more dignified calling of the theater. Even though Griffith is usually mentioned as one of the half-dozen all-time great filmmakers, he never completely overcame his initial notion of the inferiority of film, largely because he lived in a culture that *did* feel that films were inferior to the stage.

The arrival of film as a serious art and as a subject of research in graduate schools and research centers has been slow, and many church people still feel a sense of uneasiness like that which plagued Griffith. But the churchgoer need only ask himself "what influences the public?" and he will find film high on the list. And he need only attend a film like Francois Truffaut's *The Wild Child* or Nicholas Roeg's *Walkabout* to find that no other medium has quite the same power to grip the emotion and transform the mind. Films are important, and churchgoers must develop an appreciation of that importance.

This leads directly to the second objection some might have to our suggestion of film education within the church. Why should the church involve itself in this education? Granted the importance of film education, is it not a secular pursuit? Could it not be accomplished more effectively in schools and other nonreligious settings?

These objections would have been more valid in times before there was a clear acceptance of the fact that the reality of God is to be found in all realms of life and not merely within religious realms. It would be irresponsible for the church of today to ignore an influential medium like film in its educational program on the basis of a simplistic division between the religious and the secular. Needless to say, there will inevitably be a theological dimension to the film education undertaken in a church. We shall discuss the tensions that this leads to in the next chapter.

Our concern in this book is more with the film medium than with the nature of the church. But a brief outline of the functions of the church may prove helpful in answering the question of why the church should be concerned with film education at all. This outline might be summed up by a rule of thumb that I have found helpful: wherever men hurt or rejoice, there is the place for the church to be at work.

As I evaluate the church today, it seems to me that it needs to perform at least three functions:

(1) The church is a *sustaining community.* This function includes the tasks that are traditionally subsumed under the headings of pastoral care, preaching, and education. The church has a legitimate concern for sustaining its membership through periods of stress and growth.

(2) The church is an *agent of change*. There are times when the church must do things that enable it, as a corporate body, to influence the decisions of the larger society and bring about changes of behavior and structure.

(3) The church is a *sensitizing community*. In addition to sustaining its members, the church needs to bring them information that will make them sensitive to issues and concerns. Doing this may well lead the church and its members to act as an agent of change, but the function of sensitizing is essentially one of exposing people to issues and problems. Film education falls into this third category. Church members must be exposed to the importance of film and brought to a point where they can receive the value of a film.

Let us look now at some general guidelines and resources for film education in the church. First of all, it is important when undertaking this sensitizing function to be sensitive to the various stages of film appreciation displayed by the members of the church. There will be young college students well versed in the works of Godard and Bergman; but there will also be older adults who have not seen a film in twenty years or more. Failure to recognize these differences can lead to unpleasant and unnecessary tensions.

For example, what I would say about Ingmar Bergman's *The Silence* to a film study group within the church would be said from the perspective of one who accepts film as an art form and Bergman as an important artist. I would ask such a group to look at this picture cinematically. What is Bergman's vision? How has he used the medium of film to communicate that vision? How does this film fit into Bergman's total cinematic output?

Discussing the same film among a group of church people not oriented to film would pose entirely different problems. I know of one young pastor who was transferred to another parish because he included *The Silence* as part of a film series in a large city church. The choice of this film for the particular audience was indeed imprudent. The pastor ought to have known that the artistic vision of sexuality Bergman presents in *The Silence* would not communicate to that particular audience.

Film education has only recently been recognized as a concern of the church. An illustration of this new concern is the change in the Legion of Decency. Its power had gradually disappeared over the years as Roman Catholics came more and more to look on the decision of whether or not to attend a given film as a matter of individual conscience, not something to be determined by the church hierarchy. Its power waning, the Legion changed its name to the National Catholic Office for Motion Pictures. Its image began to shift from that of an agency making moral judgments to that of one offering educational guidance. It lent support to the National Center for Film Study (now a nondenominational office) in developing study materials for churches that wanted to study pictures with greater seriousness and needed more than a simple listing of ratings for this.

This is not to say that film education has arisen simply as a desperation move born out of a loss of ecclesiastical power. For the last two decades, while the church was slowly losing its influence over the Hollywood product, there have always been some church people studying film as an art form, discovering insights into the human condition and commentaries on society. The 16-millimeter film rental market began slowly, but by the beginning of the 1960s more and more companies were busy supplying quality films to local churches. "Sunday Night at the Movies" became a standard practice in many parishes.

Expanding on this showing of a feature film on Sunday night, some churches have begun such film educational projects as studying in detail the films of a given director. A favorite for this purpose is Ingmar Bergman because of the obvious manner in which he struggles with faith and doubt. Since the earliest concern that the church displayed for film was with its lack of morality, it is natural that the churchgoers involved in film education today still evidence a good deal of concern for the moral content of film. The "generalist" in film education will probably show his congregation films that illuminate moral points or illustrate social concerns. This leads to the use of artistically inferior films like *Butterfield 8* (prostitution) and *Raisin in the Sun* (race) to demonstrate a religious point the pastor wants to make. Increasingly, however, the churchmen who use films are insisting that the pictures they show be artistically valid as well as socially relevant.

Another method of film education is the showing of short films to a group in the church (young people or married couples) or to the entire congregation, after which the audience discusses what they have seen. Film distributors report that among the films most frequently requested for this purpose are *The Stringbean, Occurrence at Owl Creek Bridge, Timepiece, A Chairy Tale, Neighbors,* and *The Pusher.* All these short films are artistically strong and also lend themselves readily to discussion of specific issues — loneliness, war, capital punishment, brotherhood, and materialism.

Guides for films of this sort have been developed by the National Center for Film Study, a nondenominational research and materials center begun in 1964 as a film education arm of the Roman Catholic diocese of Chicago. For many years this Center has been the major producer and supplier of study materials for film in church use. One of the men who founded the Center, Mr. Henry Herx, is now attached to the National Catholic Office for Motion Pictures in New York as education editor. Thanks in part to the educational emphasis he has supplied, NCOMP represents much more than the Legion of Decency under a new name. While the office continues to rate films as to their suitability for different age groups, its concern is largely with education, a concern implemented by an attractive monthly newsletter discussing current cinematic releases, in part to point out moral weaknesses, but more importantly to educate Roman Catholics as to the artistic merit of particular films.

The shift to considering film as an art form can also be seen in the Protestant churches. The office of the Broadcasting and Film Commission of the National Council of Churches, located in New York City, is responsible for producing radio, television, and film programs for the NCC, but it also devotes considerable time to film education. Part of the Broadcasting and Film Commission's education program is a film awards program that annually selects films of outstanding merit artistically and cites these pictures publicly. NCOMP has also been giving awards to motion pictures, and for the past several years the two offices have presented their awards at joint ceremonies. At one of these occasions Director Arthur Penn thanked the churchmen for the recognition they had given his picture *Bonnie and Clyde.* Penn said that one reason the award meant so much to him was that it indicated that the church understood "what we were trying to do."

Understanding what a film artist is communicating is the purpose of such awards; each year the awards committees seek those pictures that make a serious effort to grapple with issues that also concern the church. But the films must also have artistic merit, which is one reason for the importance of the recognition given *Bonnie and Clyde.* Here is a film that is both a stunning cinematic achievement and a searing indictment of the American preoccupation with violence as a means to every end. The church award "educated" the church public regarding the value of this film.

Another part of the Protestant film education program is *Film Information,* a monthly publication administered by the Broadcasting and Film Office of the NCC. *Film*

Information's reviews are written by church leaders and film critics. Most theatrical films in current release are covered. The reviews, ranging in length from a sentence to a page, are directed to church members who have a more-than-average interest in film, and they have been filling a need expressed by these people for advance information about pictures for their own guidance as well as for their children.

The church interest in film as film is paralleled and encouraged by the growing interest among younger people in the medium. The college students who thrilled to *The Pawnbroker* in 1965 are now young parents (and ministers) in churches, and they want to know more about what makes a film like that such a compelling document. This has led to church film study groups, to special series of films for Lent or Advent, and to the use of films in the Sunday worship service. One midwestern youth group, for example, spent from Friday night to Sunday morning viewing short films, and planning how they would conduct the Sunday morning worship service that was to close their retreat. They selected *The Stringbean* as the "sermon." Participants reported that the story of a lonely woman growing a bean in a pot moved many of the youngsters to tears, something that had not happened through a sermon in anyone's memory.

Some seminaries have included film study in the curriculum. Claremont School of Theology, a United Methodist seminary near Los Angeles, offers a degree in theology and the arts, with heavy concentration on film. This program involves students in detailed study of film as an art form, in the language and history of film, and in an examination of the theological implications of film statements. Study groups of older ministers are also studying film as part of their continuing education program, recognizing that their seminary education in the 1930s and 1940s

failed to equip them to interpret a medium that is becoming increasingly important in contemporary culture. The realization is growing that a church member can attend the showing of a film like *The Greatest Story Ever Told* and fail to find any authentic religious content in it. But he can see a film like *Midnight Cowboy* and witness a revelation of love that provides him with insight into his own possibilities and needs. The film industry does not yet fully realize what is happening to its former enemy, the church. Church magazines now carry reviews of current films, but even when he reads a favorable review of *Little Big Man* or *Patton* in such a periodical, the film distributor has difficulty believing that church leaders can be interested in pictures that do not have a "religious" theme or talk about the beauties of family life. Old images die hard, but the film education movement within the churches in the United States is working to create a new image of the church-film dialogue.

Chapter 2

DO-IT-YOURSELF
FILM CRITICISM

A Critical Methodology

I recall once having been offered tickets to a musical
concert by a friend in college. Looking forward to filling
an evening with culture, I accepted enthusiastically. I
asked my friend who would be featured at the concert; and
he answered, "Sir Thomas Beecham." Innocently, I asked,
"What instrument does he play?" My friend, a staunch
admirer of Sir Thomas, the great *conductor,* quietly took
the tickets out of my hand and said firmly, "You don't
deserve to go."

Despite my lamentable ignorance, the snobbish remark
of my friend really missed the point. Appreciation of
"culture" is not the prerogative of an elite few who have
earned some kind of "right." This should be borne in mind
in this chapter as we discuss more specific ways in which
film education can sensitize individuals in the church to
the medium of cinema. Intelligent appreciation of cinema
is not something that is necessarily limited to a minority
who have special and exceptional qualifications. To be
sure, some orientation is required, some familiarity with
the medium. But gaining and developing that appreciation
is part of film education. There is no body of information
that one needs for this ahead of time: the only prerequisite
is an open mind.

In this chapter we shall be concerned with providing a
methodology for attaining that kind of orientation to film.

We should note at the outset that what we are talking about is, precisely, a methodology. It is not a set of canons that one can apply to a given film and determine whether it is a "good" film or a "bad" film. This is not to say that there are no such standards. The point is that film perception is a very subjective matter. What prevents complete anarchy in this area is that there does seem to be enough commonality among viewers to attain general agreement on a large number of films. But the methodology we shall be developing in this chapter is designed to take full account of this relativity of personal judgment. It is designed as a framework, a structure. In that sense it is functional — more a tool than an eternal verity. To say it another way, instead of providing answers, it aims at helping the viewer to ask the right questions.

To a great extent, this methodology has evolved as a defense mechanism from my contacts with church members. The average person I encounter as I lecture about film to church groups has little interest in film as an art form. He is accustomed to receiving film as he has been trained to receive all forms of communication — entirely in terms of linearity. What matters most to him, in other words, is the story-*line* — the plot — and the dialogue. His expectation when he goes to see a film is that it moves from A to B to C to D in orderly progression. Films like *Petulia* or *2001: A Space Odyssey* or *Little Big Man,* which do not meet that criterion, merely irritate him.

A gulf seems to exist between films that are critically acclaimed and films that are widely appreciated by the man-in-the-street and the churchgoer-in-the-pew. It is my contention that this gulf need not exist, that it can be bridged by the approach of film education, and that the sort of film education required is not impossible or even unrealistic.

There is one further point to be made before we talk about the methodology itself. We have been concerned thus far with the particular relationship between church and film. Our methodology aims at taking films seriously as works of art; that is, we want to look at "film as film." How are these two to be correlated? What does it mean for a Christian critic to be concerned with "film as film"?

In the first place, no critic — Christian or otherwise — comes to a work of art without bringing his own perspective to it. The Christian critic's approach is informed by the Christian faith, and the presuppositions of that faith will be operative in his criticism. Yet, if he is to respect secular structures and patterns for their potential of revelation, he must attend to them as they are presented, rather than force them to fit a preconceived religious mold.

Consider an obvious example. When a Christian film critic examines a film whose subject matter has to do with sexuality, the critic will have to confront the vision of sexuality projected to him by the filmmaker. If he is blinded to that vision ahead of time by his own moral principles and a bias against any understanding of sexuality not in keeping with his own, he cannot attend to the filmmaker's vision. So he will be resisting the possibility of insight or understanding that the filmmaker might provide. Of course, the vision of sexuality projected by many commercial films is easily rejected as superficial, phony, and distorted, but in the process of rejecting such a vision the Christian critic must first weigh the artistic manner in which that vision is projected and only secondarily ask whether or not it agrees with his own vision of sexuality. In this way he will be taking seriously — and judging on its own merits — a work of film art.

To put it another way, the critic must be careful to sort out his personal reactions to a film. I recall an enthusiastic review I once wrote about a film dealing with World War II. A film teacher read the review and commented, "You are not reviewing the picture; you are reviewing the war." He was right. My teen-age memories of the glamour of

World War II make me susceptible to any film that evokes those recollections. I lose my judgment in this area unless I make a conscious effort to consider the film in terms other than nostalgic.

In the same way, it is possible to make moralistic judgments against a film because it happens to violate our understanding of moral behavior. Whatever the merit of the work at hand, this kind of criticism will register a negative reaction if profanity, nudity, or overt immorality appears on screen. This may or may not be good moralism; it *is* bad criticism. This does not mean that the critic remains neutral in his critical evaluation. Rather, it suggests that he be aware of the material before him and aware of his own presuppositions so that the relationship between viewer and film will operate with a maximum of openness.

Facing this problem is not easy for the Christian critic who is operating in an ecclesiastical context, for he must always live in the tension between the aesthetic dimension of the film as an art form and the religious judgment the church can and must make regarding the effect of the film on individuals and society. It is a tension between examining a film from the perspective of cinema and viewing it as a church leader. Obviously he can never abandon either of these two points of view, but he should always be conscious that he is approaching his subject within the context of this tension.

This is not to suggest that it is only in ecclesiastical contexts that films can be viewed noncinematically. For example, when a motion picture is discussed on a late-night television talk show, it is being discussed within a secular context, but what is said are things that a nonfilm audience would talk about. That is, the film is being discussed as a social phenomenon rather than as a work of cinematic art. The talk-show host's sly grin lets his audience know what he thinks of "naughty pictures." *I Am Curious (Yellow)* — to take a recent example — is an important little film, mediocre in quality but interesting as an attempt at documentary and also important as a part of the corpus of a specific filmmaker. The talk-show approach to this film, however, is concerned only with the sex depicted in it. Such a concern ignores its cinematic qualities — good and bad — and looks at the film only as a social phenomenon. It is this approach that the church has relied on too often, looking on film from the outside as a phenomenon that is largely detrimental to society.

It is important for us to be aware of this distinction between looking at film as a social phenomenon and looking at it as cinematic art so that we can be clear as to the language we arc using when we discuss a picture. Alfred North Whitehead tells of going to a matinee performance of *Carmen* with a lady and her ten-year-old niece. After the performance, the two adults were discussing *Carmen* on the sidewalk, and the girl asked her aunt, "Do you think that those were really *good* people?"

Neither the aunt nor Whitehead had contemplated the answer to that particular question because it was not relevant to the opera as they had experienced it. Their concern had been with the merit of the performance — its "good"-ness — and the significance of the artistic work. Similarly, in the case of a popular medium like film, we find many church people far too anxious to raise the niece's question about morals rather than the primary question of the merit of the work at hand.

Film education undertaken in a church community will quite naturally have a theological dimension. But this does not mean that the film as art will be forced to conform to certain preconceived religious notions. Rather, the film as art should be permitted to be itself, a vehicle through which the artist presents his vision. The task of the churchman is then to evaluate that vision in the light of his own understanding, informed by the Christian faith.

My first intimations of the methodology to be discussed

in the remainder of this chapter probably date back to my viewing of Antonioni's *L'Avventura* in 1960. I went to this picture as a member of a church group. Our decision to go was probably the result of the local paper's having described the film as "important." We wanted above all in those early days of "secularity" to be relevant. *L'Avventura* begins with the disappearance of a young girl on a lonely island. Her friends look for her, and failing to find her on the island they extend their search to the mainland. Her fiancé and a second girl travel through lonely and bleak Italian countryside looking, but more importantly, falling in love. Soon it becomes apparent that they have lost interest in their search, and they are barely able to maintain interest in one another. The film closes with an intense scene of reconciliation, the girl's hand reaching out to touch the head of her lover.

In the discussion that followed our viewing of the film two differing opinions quickly became apparent. Some of the people kept wondering what happened to the first girl; others argued that what happened to her was not really of any importance. I found myself in the second group, unconcerned with the so-called plot. What mattered was the immediate experience that Antonioni shared: two people groping for some meaning in the midst of a loveless existence. Seeing the film as experience, I was concerned not with the plot or story but with the vision of life that the filmmaker projected through his film, with or without plot.

This concept has not been easy to convey to many casual filmgoers. My methodology for perceiving film grew from a desire to share this sense of film as experience, and not simply as a story on film. In the following pages I shall outline this methodology, apply it to some specific types of film, and conclude by using it to evaluate a number of individual pictures.

Imagine that our experience of receiving film ranges

from one end of a continuum of perception to the other. At one end of this continuum is experience that picks up what the film is *about* — such things as its plot line, character development, message. At the other end of the continuum we perceive what the film *is* — what it projects in and of itself. There are various terms we could use to point out the differences between these two kinds of perception. We might refer to the former as objective and the latter as subjective perception. Or we might talk about the intellectual and intuitive modes of perception. We shall use the word "discursive" to describe our perception at the end of the continuum that has to do with what the film *is about,* and the word "presentational" to delineate the perception at the other end of the continuum — what the film *is*. The advantage of these terms over the others we have mentioned is that they do not carry the same freight of meaning from psychology and philosophy.*

Note that these are not terms that are applied to a film itself, but terms that refer to the viewer's perception of a film. Were we to call a given film "discursive" or "presentational" we would be giving that picture a final and enclosing framework that would limit the possibilities of what it is and what it can do. Furthermore, the two types of perception are not mutually exclusive. It is probably the case that our perception of any film will fall somewhere between the two ends of the continuum, closer to the one or the other depending on the film involved. To the extent that films have a beginning and an ending and that they deal with people and situations, some discursive perception will always be appropriate. Only a completely abstract film could be perceived entirely on a presentational level.

*The categories suggested here are drawn from the work of Suzanne Langer, who uses them in a somewhat different fashion to distinguish the use of symbols. The meaning we attach to the two categories differs from her use; however, her insight that the presentational (or nondiscursive) symbol has its own power to formulate meaning and project it into the cognition of a viewer is the original source of my own methodology.

What do these metaphors of perception mean? What are we doing when we perceive a film discursively? When we perceive a film at this level, we focus largely on the material before us in an audiovisual sense, allowing the content to point beyond itself to a story, a principle, a propaganda point, a period of history. Narrative documentary films and most films made from novels lend themselves to this mode of perception. The viewer's reception of these films will be located, for the most part (not entirely, to be sure), toward the discursive end of the perception continuum.

On the other hand, when a film reaches us primarily at the presentational end of the continuum, we are not so much concerned with the information it may impart or the plot it may develop. We focus instead on the vision that the film projects. Because the film lends itself readily to this kind of perception, it has a greater potential for involvement with the viewer. It is more personal. It functions at the level of engagement. Whether or not it does engage a particular viewer will depend on the extent to which the viewer can relate it to his own life, his own "biography." The success or failure of the film for the particular viewer, then, will depend on a number of variables, including taste, context, form, and structure.

We suggested that some films lend themselves to being perceived more discursively than others. Though such a film presents a vision of reality in its form and its content, that vision takes second place to the discursive data. The ability of this film to hold a person's interest will vary from viewer to viewer and from time to time, depending on the viewer's prior interest in the subject matter at hand.

For example, a film made by an insurance company to train its salesmen will be of intense interest to the salesman at a conference, especially if he is going to sell on a commission. He will follow closely the simple, one-two-three discursive content of the film because he wants to pick up what it says for his own benefit. But the man who is not an insurance salesman will not watch such a film with much interest, because it cannot hold his interest discursively, and the film's presentational content is so secondary as to be negligible.

At another level, consider biblical spectaculars. As long as interest was high in the facts of biblical history *per se* — what we might call "biblical information" — interest was high in these "beards and bathrobe epics." Today the biblical spectacular (most recently *The Greatest Story Ever Told*) is box office poison. Its discursive content holds little interest for a secular public. Its presentational message — its ability to present itself with such potency that it convicts and converts — is almost nonexistent if some external interpretation is not added to point to its relevancy for a period other than the first century. Surface content is its major concern, which explains the huge sums of money that movie studios used to take great pride in spending on "authentic" detail. First-century soldiers had to wear uniforms that were in fact worn in the first century; any coins used had to be first-century coins. But widespread lack of interest in the discursive content of films that exploit such devices makes "authentic" biblical spectaculars a waste of the filmmaker's money today.

If a film requires perception only at the discursive end of the continuum, it will quickly jade the viewer unless its discursive content is new material. This holds true even for explicit sex films, a fact confirmed by the findings of the President's Commission on Obscenity and Pornography. In its report the Commission noted that, in a controlled test, college students soon became tired of looking at hard-core visual pornography. The students were sent to a closed room, where there was a choice of magazines they could read — a sampling of hard-core pornography and a variety of magazines such as *Time, Life,* and the like. In the early stages of the experiment the students invariably picked up the pornography immediately, but as the test was repeated, they soon grew tired of the visual sex and started reading the other magazines available.

Whether it be to selling insurance, growing corn, or solving a perplexing whodunit, the content of a film that is perceived at the discursive end of the continuum must point the viewer beyond itself to something that is important to him. Otherwise the film cannot hold his interest or attention. Still, someone may argue, are there not a considerable number of films available that appeal to discursive perception? Why should anyone bother with films that require perception at the presentational end of the continuum we have described? Let us consider this question from three different angles.

In the first place, every film we see is a reality in its own right. Even the documentary film shown on television, though it deals with "real" events (in contrast to acted-out events) is *what it is,* and is not an exact reproduction of what it presents. Selectivity was involved in shooting the film, editing it, and arranging it in the form it is seen. Now some films have a distinct vision designed to engage and involve the viewer with an awareness beyond the mere surface reporting of events. To talk about this kind of vision is to raise the elusive and difficult question of what art is. It is not our purpose here to answer that question in any detail, but it is possible at least to say that, over the years, those works of creativity that have commanded respect as "artistic" are works that have *engaged* the viewer or reader. A film that attempts to project a vision distinctively its own is a film that has the potential for engaging the viewer. In terms of the methodology we have been outlining, such a film is to be perceived at the presentational end of the continuum. The viewer who chooses to ignore the possibilities of this kind of perception — the viewer who wants only to watch films discursively — will be shutting himself off from significant artistic engagement.

A second reason for opening oneself to perception at the presentational end of the continuum has to do with the obvious fact that at this point in our cultural history an increasing number of films seem deliberately to be avoiding familiar principles of plot and logic. Those viewers who are geared to perceiving films only discursively, for whom the "linear" — A-B-C-D — progression is the only one that makes sense will find it nearly impossible to accept many contemporary films, which may go D-A-C and omit B entirely, for example. Antonioni's *Blow-Up* and *Zabriskie Point* both shift back and forth between fantasy and reality to such an extent that the viewer is never absolutely certain which is which. *Blow-Up* has a limited plot line: it is possible to make some tentative suggestion as to what it is "about." Certainly it has to do with a young photographer at loose ends with himself in a London flat. But Antonioni's style is to be deliberately vague with his plot, thus forcing the viewer to perceive the film toward the presentational end of the continuum. To receive maximum benefit from the film, the viewer must attend to Antonioni's vision and reckon with the suggestion that the separation between fantasy and reality is not as striking or important as our rational age assumes. If the viewer finds Antonioni's vision unimportant or poorly conveyed, that of course is his prerogative. But if he makes that kind of criticism of the film, he will at least have dealt with the material at hand in terms of its original intention; and his criticism will be to the point.

A film like *Z* tries another approach to the distinction between reality and unreality. The death of a Greek pacifist leader is reproduced in several versions, suggesting that how he died depends entirely on how his death is seen. Walter Kerr, drama critic for the *New York Times,* sees this same mixture of rational and irrational in contemporary drama. What he has said about this kind of play can be applied equally to contemporary films. Noting that the

new form of drama is largely plotless, Kerr writes:

> No one need like all the plays in which this kind of work is done; I suppose I must dislike half of them heartily.... Old norms tend to shatter under such stretching, and one must go by instinct again; but that is a pleasantly personal and directly engaged way of responding to a play, and it conforms fairly closely to our out-of-theater lives.... If I had to sum up the whole business in the fastest conceivable way, I'd simply say that we have moved from logical theater into a phenomenological one. Look at the thing hard. What thing? Everything. And don't try to say what it is until you've had it long enough in hand to know its tricks.*

Film, like drama, is steering away from the logical, reflecting the fact that contemporary life no longer lends itself easily to strict logical interpretation. This does not mean that we are to cease being logical beings. To do so would negate civilization. But it does mean that, as a more sensory-oriented culture, we must be prepared to receive openly what is presented before we make our final judgments about it.

In order to get at our third answer to the question "Why bother with films that have to be perceived at the presentational end of the continuum?" let us consider a motion picture made in a day when a film's story-line was more important that it is now, *From Here to Eternity*. This film is perceived primarily at the discursive end of the continuum, because its primary purpose is to develop plot and character. The film tells a story. The viewers become involved in what happens to the people described. Since the focus is on plot, what *From Here to Eternity* presents in terms of attitudes toward Army life, marriage, and conformity is secondary. According to our methodology, *From Here to Eternity* must be perceived, primarily, at this level of plot and character interaction. What the film presents as a vision is at a secondary level, and this vision does not have the power to engage or involve the viewer, because his major concern is what happens to *these* particular individ-

*In *The New York Times*, August, 1968.

39

uals, not what happens to man in general, or even to soldiers in prewar Pearl Harbor.

The discursiveness of a film like this one is what permits us to "escape" into it as a diversion. This characteristic of films is what the general public most expects. When we view a film as escapism, we allow ourselves to be concerned, in however limited a way, about nonexistent characters or stereotypes — the lonely soldier, the wronged wife. By contrast, a film that engages us at the presentational end of the continuum offers us a vision from the filmmaker that requests an acceptance or rejection in and of itself. Antonioni's *Blow-Up* presents a personal vision of contemporary humanity. Fellini's *Satyricon* offers us a personal vision of contemporary humanity in a pre-Christian setting. Both of these films, by offering such a vision, set up the possibility of our saying yes or no to that vision.

Is it possible to "escape" into a film that demands our perception at the presentational end of the continuum? Not really, for "escaping into a film" means moving away from that which deeply concerns us. *The Pawnbroker* requires a personal decision from the viewer because it projects a vision regarding the nature of man that has to be accepted or rejected. Those who walked away from *Blow-Up* with the complaint that it was stupid and meaningless may have been expressing their rejection of its vision. On the other hand, they may also have been reflecting dissatisfaction at being unable to "escape" into the movie. In terms of our methodology, the latter group had gone astray by perceiving discursively that which ought to have been perceived presentationally.

The goal of the methodology we have been outlining is to set up overall metaphors that will enable the film viewer to break away from a plot-oriented literary pattern and receive film as film. It is especially valuable for those who have been accustomed to seeing every film as a story *about* something or somebody. It may also help provide structure for those who have broken away from the plot-oriented pattern, who have learned to *experience* film rather than merely *see* it, but have had difficulty articulating their reactions to given films in these terms.

The question "what is this film *about*?" is, we have suggested, one that is directed to discursive perception. The experimental filmmaker Tom DeWitt was recently interviewed on CBS television and asked by an interviewer exactly what his films were *about*. DeWitt replied:

> "You ask me what my films are *about*? My films are *about* five minutes long. My films are *a bout* between imagination and reality. My films are *about* all I do."

DeWitt is doing more here than making bad puns. He is really responding to a discursive question with presentational answers. From his point of view, the experimental pictures he is making do not have an *about* quality. He considers them as statements, projecting his private vision through a particular medium. Of course, the viewer can see DeWitt films and make his own observations regarding their "aboutness," but in all likelihood his observations would have little to do with the essential dynamic of the films.

This is what our methodology guards against — automatic evaluation of a film in terms of the question "What is it about?" It insists that we distinguish between a film's overall vision and the structural plot through which that vision is projected. Furthermore, it requires us to acknowledge a greater degree of relativity of personal judgment in film criticism, for, as we have suggested, presentational perception in particular has a great deal to do with the biography of the viewer making the judgment. In the remainder of this chapter, we shall look at some further distinctions that may be helpful in applying the discursive-presentational methodology, concluding with a look at how all of this bears on the question of relativity and absolute judgments in film criticism.

Discussing our reception of painting, John Hospers suggests that there are three dimensions to the aesthetic experience: reception in terms of *surface,* in terms of *form,* and in terms of *life-values.* How might this be applied to our reception of film?

Surface experience, in this scheme, is that which immediately strikes the senses of the viewer — color, shape, sound. The form of the film represents the manner in which this surface material is organized — framing, movement within a frame, editing, pacing, rhythm. Finally, the dimension of life-values introduces the preconceptions brought to the experience of the film by the viewer. The film itself possesses its own life-values, and these will be received and measured in terms of the life-values of the viewer.

How does this work with a specific film? Consider Agnes Varda's film *Le Bonheur* ("Happiness"). It is superbly photographed. Its color reflects the soft pastels of a spring afternoon and the dark hues of a rich autumn. The film opens in the spring and follows a small family — man, wife, and young daughter — through what is apparently a happy existence in a suburb of Paris. During the summer the husband meets another woman and takes her as mistress. He tells his wife about this arrangement, which she appears to accept as something that can provide an added dimension of joy to their marriage. But in the next scene we discover that the wife has committed suicide. The husband's initial reaction is one of shock and chagrin. After his wife's funeral, however, he marries his former mistress; and the film ends with the same happy images that it began with, surrounded by fall colors. Only the wives have changed.

The surface evaluation of *Le Bonheur* will take into account the lush colors of the film and its immediate sense of urban, suburban, and rural life, which the filmmaker skillfully manipulates in order to convey the notion of contentment and happiness. When we evaluate the picture's form, we will note the ease and slow pace, the graceful movement of the picture between scenes of apparent joy, except for the sudden moment of suicide.

When we introduce the third dimension of the aesthetic experience as Hospers sees it, life-values, we confront immediately Miss Varda's view of marriage. Our own life-values must interact with the life-values she projects in the film. Discursively, it would seem that she is suggesting that the wife was foolish, that her suicide was an inappropriate response to her husband's adultery. But presentationally there is a different vision altogether. Miss Varda's film portrays the world as seen through the eyes of the husband. Every scene is deliberately made to be one of happiness, for this is the way the world hits the man. His selfish use of two women at the same time appears, to his limited vision, to be a reasonable manner of operation. The key to the film is the suicide, which seems to be so inconsistent with all that has preceded it. This is the only touch of reality that gets through to the husband. He cannot deny his wife's death: it is a reality that cannot be adjusted to fit his self-centered universe. Miss Varda has this awareness repeated several times in slow-motion as the husband picks up his wife's dead body. But once the funeral is past he re-enters his own world and goes on seeing all others as available to serve him and make him happy.

Our life-values are brought into play when we see this film. We are forced to ask why the filmmaker treats the adultery so slightly, for our life-values do not permit such casual treatment of the marriage relationship. It is possible for some filmmakers to have this kind of casual attitude towards adultery and to project their attitude through their films. But Miss Varda's intent in *Le Bonheur* is not to have us see adultery as a happy arrangement, but to see it only as an arrangement of utter selfishness not recognized by the husband. Our life-value evaluation of this picture forces us to measure our understanding of adultery against that of Miss Varda's. Viewed discursively, on the surface level, her film seems to condone adultery because the plot requires it. But presentationally an entirely different understanding emerges. And this understanding is apparent to us only after we have measured the beauty and gentleness of the surface and form of *Le Bonheur* against the life-values of the director's vision.

Another way of getting at what we are trying to say in our methodological distinction between discursive and presentational perception is suggested by William Kloman, who uses the language of the youth culture to distinguish between "understanding" a picture and "groovin' " with it. To "groove" with a picture, the viewer is obligated to yield himself to the flow of activity around him. He must be "with it" as a phonograph needle is "with" the record groove, responding to its microscopic impressions. In this way he can receive the full vision of the work before him.

To "groove" with a film does not mean that we give up making moral judgments about it, but that we postpone those judgments until we have let the film have its final say to us. We will naturally be responding to the film as it progresses, and there will always be a correlation between our response to people and events in everyday life and in fictional viewing. But to the extent that a film is meant to be received presentationally, to that extent it is essential that we learn to "groove" with it.

There is a danger here of overdoing a good thing. To confine ourselves entirely to "groovin'," with no effort at understanding, is as irresponsible as demanding that everything before us yield immediately to a logical understanding. But an emphasis on "groovin' " is especially important in contemporary American culture as an antidote to the widely held notion that any work of art can be interpreted in such a way that its "meaning" is reducible

44

to a single declarative sentence. Trained to look at works of art in that way, many Americans have come to insist on functional art. Thus, Kloman writes, "a lush image of daffodils could be reduced to a statement from the student that 'it says the poet's girl friend has yellow hair.' Gradually we were taught that if this is all the poet wishes to say, then it is best that he simply tell us that his girl is a blonde." As a result of this kind of pragmatically oriented training, Kloman concludes, "people grew up with their artistic receptors atrophied beyond repair."*

It is against this handicap that we work to provide an openness to films that — whatever their inadequacies — have the potential to provide "groovin'" experiences. I remember an evening in Chicago when my wife and I saw a performance of Harold Pinter's *The Homecoming*. Stunned by the evocative power of the drama, we were leaving the theater when a woman behind us announced loudly, "Well, I don't like it because I don't understand it." She might have "liked" it, however, had she made an effort to "groove" with Pinter's vision of noncommunication in contemporary life, rather than trying to "understand" it. To look for meaning and plot in a Pinter play is to guarantee confusion and frustration. *The Homecoming* deliberately avoids a reasonable plot with normal interchanges because Pinter wants to twist reality out of line. He sets up a conventional situation — a father living in London with two sons — and has a third son return from America with his new wife. Like life, this promises some logic, some resolution, but like life, it does not provide this. Instead, what follows is a bizarre situation in which participants talk past one another, leaving those aching voids in the air that reflect what is not said or cannot be felt by those portrayed on stage. But the audience feels and senses — if it is receptive — that more is at stake here than the relationship between this particular son and his family. Pinter

*In *The New York Times*, June 12, 1968.

45

shares a vision through the structure of this play, evoking an awareness of the terrible pain caused by the absence of communication between those who should have been close and intimate with one another. He shares this vision not by talking *about* the absence of communication but by *presenting* that absence.

An audience that has had, in Kloman's words, its "artistic receptors atrophied beyond repair" will simply not be prepared to receive Pinter. Personally, I feel that these people are missing an important experience. This, we should note, is a personal bias, not a final statement of truth. There are no absolutes in art reception. Applied to films, this means that if you and I view the same film, and that film strikes me and leaves you cold, or vice versa, a number of things may be deduced about you and me and the film, but what cannot be deduced is that one of us is "right" and the other is "wrong." Now there may be something like "community" or "subgroup" consensus about a particular film, and it could be said that if a subgroup in society generally agrees on the merit of a particular film, and one member of that subgroup disagrees, he is wrong within or in terms of the values of his subgroup. But that is a form of "wrongness" that is entirely relative to the subgroup itself.

A film like *Sound of Music,* for example, strikes me as a shallow rendition of a familiar theme. It is pleasant enough, but it is certainly not gripping and evocative enough to send me out into the streets singing its praises. This is my subjective artistic judgment, a judgment apparently not shared by a large number of filmgoers, who have made *Sound of Music* the number one grossing picture of all time. By the beginning of 1971, this picture had grossed almost $100 million, passing *Gone With the Wind,* the former champion, by several million dollars. Film critics generally agree that both of these films are below average as works of film art. They are unimaginative, develop obvious plots, and depend on stereotype characters. But both were successful. Why?

Film companies would like to know the precise answer to that question, so they could repeat the success. Many tried, following the surprising reception of *Sound of Music*. The companies who flooded the market with *Star, Paint Your Wagon, Dr. Doolittle,* and *The Happiest Millionaire* — to name only a few of the failures — thought they could come up with their own *Sound of Music* to shore them up financially. None succeeded. The secret of the *Sound of Music* is really simple: the picture found an audience that wanted that particular film at that particular time. It is known that most of the tickets were sold to older viewers, many of whom spend most of their entertainment time in front of television. *Sound of Music* set off a certain resonance in older audiences. It was a picture that even nonfilmgoers felt they should attend. It almost became one of the badges of cultural honor within this particular subculture that one had gone to see *Sound of Music*.

A few years later, a totally different segment of the filmgoing public responded to *Bonnie and Clyde* and *The Graduate*. This was a younger audience, different from that which had flocked to *Sound of Music*. These two pictures had struck a responsive chord in a viewing subculture that was aware of the violence in American life and of the generation gap. I heard an older woman say that she hated *The Graduate* because it ridiculed everything in life that her family considered important. Precisely. That is exactly why the film was so effective for younger audiences. It was one of the first pictures to capture on film the deep sense of alienation that youngsters feel when they compare their own world-views with the packaged, limited world-views of their elders.

The viewers who see these films find that their "biographies" are touched in a significant way by the vision of

47

the film. A resonance is set up that rings true to a particular subculture, and this resonance may or may not be related to the artistic merit of a film. *The Graduate,* for example, can be criticized for being two different pictures, for providing stereotypes of the young and the old, for catering to the younger audience. In short, it lacked honesty. Yet this was of no concern to the subculture that responded to it.

From my critical point of view, a viewer's presentational reception of a film reveals a great deal about his "biography." Thus, if a film presents itself to me and I reject what it presents, it will be largely because I reject the vision that is projected. But if the vision convicts me, bringing about a change − great or small − in my own vision, the film has performed a creative function. To pick up presentationally what is projected through *The Graduate* is to receive a vision of modern life as filled with emptiness. To me, the closing scene is not a "happy" ending, as many critics have suggested, but a very sad ending. Two young people, so much a product of their own times, are starting married life badly handicapped by past experiences and possessed only of a desire to rebel. It is not a happy prospect. Discursively, it appears happy − boy wins girl. But presentationally, in the light of the entire film's vision of modern life, it is sad, for the victory is a limited one.

Consider a film like *2001: A Space Odyssey,* which got an initial negative reception from the critics, but which has gone on to become a great favorite, again largely among younger viewers. I would suggest that the initial negative reaction was a discursive one. The critics were waiting for a story to emerge. When none did, they reacted negatively. Writing in *Newsweek,* Joseph Morgenstern condemned *Bonnie and Clyde* as a violent film. One week later he admitted in the same magazine that he had missed what Director Arthur Penn was saying. He now confessed that he found *Bonnie and Clyde* profoundly moving and significant. His initial reaction had been discursive, and only after he permitted the film's presentational qualities to work on him did its full impact strike him. Similarly, *2001* appears boring and plotless when first seen. The film's greatness, however, lies in the fact that it is boring and plotless on the surface, because Stanley Kubrick is saying that the technological world of the future will reduce men to robots and give robots personality and power. It is not until *2001* does its presentational work on the viewer that Kubrick's potent vision comes through.

Chapter 3

"LET THE MOTHER GO"

Blacks in American Films

Using the discursive-presentational methodology we outlined in the previous chapter, we can consider either individual films or types of film. Two areas that greatly concern today's churchgoer are race and sex. In this chapter we shall examine the treatment of Blacks in American films; in the next chapter we shall provide a more detailed study of sexuality in film. By doing so we can use this methodology and get a better insight into how films have responded to these two controversial topics.

One of my earliest "liberal" recollections is the act of carefully reading the separate "colored theater" listings in the Atlanta newspapers to see if the "colored people" (as we whites referred to them in those days) were getting to see pictures they would enjoy. I grew up in Monroe, Georgia, where the upper balcony in the local theater was segregated for Blacks. It always intrigued me — indeed, it gave me a peculiar sense of satisfaction — that in distant big cities "they" had their very own theaters. As I grew older, I began to suspect that those theaters were not very fashionable. After I became a theater doorman and budding movie buff, it became apparent that the "colored theaters" were playing strictly second-rate stuff. Occasional titles were listed that I had never heard of, which meant that these theaters were getting some pictures designed exclusively for Negro audiences.

More recently, as a film critic and teacher, I have examined in greater detail the treatment of Blacks in the films of the mid-1930s to the mid-1940s, when I was growing up, that era of tragic innocence when a generation of white Southerners grew up without questioning the myth of the inferior, happy darky, content to sit in the theater balcony or rock idly on his front porch in Shantytown.

Movies were important to us, filling in fantasies and reinforcing prejudices. The most influential picture of that period (and one of the biggest money-makers of all time) was *Gone With the Wind*. My memory of it is a pleasant one, for what I saw then was the gallant Scarlett, the brave Melanie, the handsome Rhett. To see *Gone With the Wind* today is to watch youthful racism being molded, for in this film the Hollywood pattern for handling the Negro is clearly visible. Hattie McDaniel is the strong, stern mammy, the matriarch of the clan who bosses little white missy, boxes the ears of dumb pickaninnies, and tolerates the shiftlessness of her menfolk. (How did the 13-year-old black youngsters in the balcony feel about these images? The question never occurred to me in 1942.)

Beyond the invisible men and the matriarchal women, *Gone With the Wind* provided an image of the black female that reflected and reinforced the racist upbringing of my generation. Butterfly McQueen left us with an indelible impression of the scared, stupid, younger black servant, failing to go for the doctor while Melanie is having her baby because "Lawsy, Miss Scarlett, I'se skeered of all them Yankee soldiers." And when Scarlett unwisely drives through a dark corner of the forest, she is set upon by some white ruffians. Her savior is black, a trusty old former servant. By the understood rules of Hollywood in 1939 — designed to cater to the public's racism — a black man could subdue white attackers only to defend the honor of a white woman.

Film racism antedates *Gone With the Wind* by several decades, of course. D. W. Griffith's *The Birth of a Nation,* released in 1915, probably deserves to be called the champion racist film of all time. When we see the film today it is easy to see why the picture elicited a storm of critical acclaim. It is a stunning cinematic portrayal of the Civil War and Reconstruction. At the same time it is easy to see why it aroused a great deal of hostile protest. Negroes in the film are either lustful or stupid. Griffith, a Kentuckian, depicted the rise of the Ku Klux Klan, portraying them as a heroic group of Southern gentlemen saving the South from bad "niggers" and carpetbaggers. The Blacks in the film are all portrayed by whites in dark make-up. Griffith insisted he was presenting an honest portrait, and indeed, no less a figure than President Woodrow Wilson called the film "history written in lightning." The protests were strong in major Eastern cities, but they were led by liberals who reacted more against the positive view of the Klan than against Griffith's caricatures of black people.

Perhaps Griffith was trying to atone in some way for his never-admitted racism with his classic film *Intolerance* (1916), a polemic against prejudice of all kinds. But Griffith is also responsible for another movie cliché: the wide-eyed Negro afraid of ghosts. Black people still could not get acting jobs in the movies, so, again, it is a white actor in blackface who enters a room, sees a ghost, and starts running. This cliche of the Negro male actually persisted in American filmmaking through the late 1950s. (Consider that. the late 1950s. Now that America has finally come to recognize racism as a national disorder rather than a Southern peculiarity, it is well to ponder how recently such a stereotype persisted and how Hollywood has been America's mercenary but real reflection of itself.)

In the late 1950s some changes came in the portrayal of Blacks in American cinema. But how much? Sidney Poitier emerged, not really as a black man, but as the white man's image of what a black man really ought to be. Poitier, through no fault of his own, has become *the* leading Negro actor, because he projects just the right amount of sensuality without threatening white audiences.

Poitier was made to order for the 1960s because the emerging racial revolution would no longer tolerate the strong mammy/frightened black boy syndrome. Filmmakers, well aware of their dependence on public acceptance, recognized that such prewar clichés of the Black had to go. In their place, on a guarded scale, came the polite, dignified Poitier, scoring first as a dock-worker in *Edge of the City* (where he is killed by a white tough), then as a spunky kid in *Blackboard Jungle* (a film about ghetto schools before that was a fashionable topic).

Poitier received an Academy Award for *Lilies of the Field,* a 1963 film in which he portrays a sophisticated carpenter who reluctantly agrees to build a chapel for a group of German nuns. The cautious Hollywood castration of the Negro male is evident here, for the nun is the one woman a black man can relate to with no fear of sexual implication. Poitier's first screen kiss came three years later in *Patch of Blue.* As a sophisticated, intelligent office worker, he befriends a blind girl in the park. She doesn't know he is black, which makes the nice liberal point that color is not important. When she kisses him she still doesn't know he is black, which makes the nice conservative point that a white girl would have to be blind to kiss a black man. In other words, the film lets us have it either way, which is in fact no way at all.

Scrutiny of films made since the emergence of the black man into the consciousness of the white public indicates that films in which race plays a part are still made with a white audience in mind. Filmmakers are aware of the growing Negro market, but to date they have cast Blacks timidly, allotting them only enough minor roles to be visible and only enough major roles to give the surface appearance of acceptance.

Poitier was the first major black star. Jim Brown is the second. As a former football star, Brown is well suited for action pictures. In *The Dirty Dozen* he tackled escaping Germans; in *Tick. . .Tick. . .Tick* he tackled an escaping white tough. White directors still established the tone of these films, and both aim at a careful balance that *suggests* real relevance to our problems but does not rile the customers by stirring up white racist hate or fear.

It is not difficult for a filmmaker to avoid presenting material that might disturb an audience. As a total experience — sight, sound, movement — film can either involve the audience by calling on viewers to identify with the characters in the picture; or it can illustrate its subject without asking for that kind of audience involvement. A picture that is anxious to please without disturbing talks *about* its topic, illustrating the subject with familiar and acceptable characterizations and plots. The most predictable characters in today's films dealing with race are the redneck sheriff and the brutal policeman, white ruffians who are so unattractive that all but the most fascist viewers have to reject them.

Stock characters and formula plots in films that deal with subjects other than race are disappearing in today's commercial films. Contemporary audiences demand a more artistic approach to the medium. *2001: A Space Odyssey,* as we noted in the previous chapter, has virtually no plot, yet youthful viewers "groove" with its visual excitement and philosophical probes. This newer style of filmmaking refuses merely to illustrate a subject; it seeks to present an artistic vision from a film artist. But there are almost no commercial films that succeed in presenting an artistic vision of present-day racism. Why is this? I think the answer lies in the profit-oriented perspective of an industry that dares not offend its buying public.

The hidden racist assumptions and emotions of white Americans (who make up the major ticket-buying public) must be carefully catered to in a mass-market product. The filmmaker who wants to involve viewers in an artistic vision avoids the cliche or formula plot, presenting instead a cinematic experience that envelops the viewer, forcing him to make decisions within the ambiguities of the film. I know of no better illustration of America's racist mentality than Hollywood's failure to make a mass-market film that artistically exposes the public to the guilt, fear, and hatred we presently experience.

Frankly I do not know how many black people still go to see these *illustrated* pictures of the white man's view of America's racism. But living primarily in a white culture, a black man who wants to see a movie does not really have much choice. He does not, however, have to respond to Whitey's vision the way it is illustrated. Several years ago, in the film *The Defiant Ones,* Tony Curtis and Sidney Poitier were handcuffed as escaping prisoners, hating each other but forced to travel together until they could find a hacksaw or key. At a crucial point, Poitier was getting free from their tormentors but Curtis was lagging behind. Poitier had to decide whether to reach out and save Curtis or to run. The "good" thing to do, of course, would be to save him. The predominantly black audience in the theater where I saw the picture roared its disapproval of Poitier's indecision. "Let the mother go!" one man shouted.

The industry is still trying, of course, to reach the Negro market. One way it has devised is through a slowly emerging policy of turning over major urban theaters to black audiences. The Roosevelt Theater in Chicago, for example, consistently plays the Brown-Poitier pictures, recognizing that the city is becoming predominantly black within subway distance and that white viewers are increasingly reluctant to leave the suburbs for the downtown area to see a film.

Within the larger market there is no clear pattern, as the industry seeks to walk its cautious line between relevance and profit. Since the early 1960s an increasing number of black faces have appeared in chorus lines, crowd shots, and supporting roles, reflecting an attempt to "think" black. (Of course, this kind of surface acceptance also has its disadvantages. *The Boys in the Band,* an off-Broadway play made into a movie, includes a Black among the eight homosexuals at the birthday party around which the film centers. Except for the homosexual market — which is small — most Blacks probably could have done without this token appearance.)

The race films of the 1970s continue to reflect something of the struggle Hollywood is undergoing, searching for that elusive formula that will stay in touch with today's black-white dynamics without offending. Jim Brown's best picture to date, for example, is *Tick. . .Tick . . .Tick.* (The title is meant to reflect the time-bomb character of Southern race relations.) The film is a portrayal of a contemporary Southern situation with the kind of kid-glove treatment that maximizes acceptance in both Northern ghettos and Southern small towns. As a returned war veteran (the best possible credentials), Brown runs for sheriff in a Mississippi town with a newly registered black voting majority and wins, the first Black to do so. The topic is timely, the film's treatment of it cautious and illustrative but not involving. Brown is quiet, respectable, determined, and capable. The film includes a sequence in which Brown lectures a black militant against hating the whites. His devotion to law and order as a new sheriff should quiet the fears of the most uncertain white Southern viewer. The plot is important because it represents an attempt to be relevant, even though for mass-market reasons. The defeated former sheriff finally comes through and helps the nonviolent black lawman as deputy. A local Ku Klux Klan leader tries to get rid of the new sheriff, but in the end even the KKK leader decides to take his stand with the sheriff in the name of law and order.

This kind of formula plot reveals how important mass-market filmmakers feel it is to be relevant — at a distance — without riling. Brown is costumed in tight white shirts. When he rolls out of the sheriff's car he projects great strength, but his strength is not uncoiled except in a wild fight with two black militants and in a gentle scene when he subdues a white punk. Whites in a film like *Tick. . . Tick. . .Tick* tend to fall into two categories: well-meaning community leaders or the worst kind of red-necks. The whites in the film, like Brown himself, are stereotypes.

A departure from this low-black-profile-no-violence formula comes in *The Liberation of L. B. Jones,* a film adaptation of Jesse Hill Ford's novel. Director William Wyler tries to follow the novel but gets bogged down badly with too many plot movements. Along the way, however, he does manage to project some effective vignettes of black behavior. The setting is small-town Tennessee; Jones is the black undertaker, and thus the only comparatively wealthy black man around. His "liberation" is his decision to stop running from the white man. Roscoe Lee Brown effectively plays the role of the stoic undertaker, who must pamper his black charges and pay obeisance to white red-necks.

One of the strong moments in the film comes when a toothless old black woman comes to the undertaker's office to pay on her "policy," and begs to see (again) her casket. Little insights like this into an older black culture help *Liberation,* but in the end it fails to come to terms with the issues of hatred that it dares to raise. Jones is murdered by two white policemen. His murder is avenged by a Black who remembers being beaten by one of the policemen as a 13-year-old. Lee J. Cobb plays the role of a white lawyer who lives in a big house because he learned long ago to compromise. He skillfully manipulates the low-class whites, who respect him, and they in turn keep order among the Blacks. There is the hint of further insight into Southern culture in this character, but Wyler fails to develop this in detail, which is finally what undermines this commercial attempt to handle subtle Southern racial conflict. The white lawyer is too blatant in telling the policeman he should forget about his part in Jones's murder; his liberal white nephew is too quick to walk out in disgust over this complicity; and there is finally not enough explanation as to how the murder of a prominent black undertaker could go unexamined in this racially sensitive era. What might have been an involving film ends up simply as a further illustration of the changing black mood. That is worth something, of course, but it is not enough.

Despite its potential for offending the customers, potential black involvement in violence is not as touchy a topic as black sex. The sight of flesh in film hardly bears comment these days, but the sight of black and white bare skin tumbling on bedsheets is not likely to appear very often in commercial films. Jim Brown did play a love scene with Raquel Welch in *100 Rifles,* but whatever nudity was present was left on the editing floor.

Black-white kissing is no longer taboo, but it does not feature prominently in films. (The kissing couple in *Liberation* are both unsympathetic characters.) Poitier's first kiss of a nonblind white girl came in *Guess Who's Coming to Dinner,* in which he kissed his prospective white bride in the back seat of a taxi. The scene was viewed fleetingly as the car moved away. The film was directed by Stanley Kramer, who has the commercial skill of directing controversial subjects with great public acceptance. As with Kramer's other films, this one only seems sensitive. Poitier confronts his prospective bride's liberal parents (played by Katherine Hepburn and Spencer Tracy) with his desire to marry their daughter, but Kramer merely informs us that racial intermarriage is the topic. He then focuses all the emotions of the audience on the feelings of these two middle-aged white liberals, who must decide whether the ideals of brotherhood they have taught their daughter can allow for racial intermarriage. Thus, the viewer has information about a touchy topic, but he is not confronted with the actual emotional involvement of the love affair itself, because the two young people, after that little peck in the taxi, are as proper together as two Victorian lovers. Audience identity is never with the youngsters but with the middle-aged liberal parents. All this makes a controversial experience entirely cerebral (which is probably the way most intellectual liberals prefer such matters).

Black-black lovemaking has only recently begun to appear in commercial films, and seldom does it display the drawn-out detail of white-white embraces. In *Hurry Sundown*, a bad Otto Preminger film based on a worse book, a black man and woman doff their clothing for a brief bed scene, but the moment is so swift that it is merely illustrative ("see, these people are human after all") and not involving. (Preminger also includes what perhaps may be the last ever scene of "plantation darkies" singing in the midst of their troubles, a scene so anachronistic that it alone probably sufficed to put *Hurry Sundown* on most lists of the "ten worst films of the year.")

The interracial love story in *The Great White Hope* served to illustrate the blind fury of Jack Jefferson, a black heavyweight boxing champion who used white women as an instrument of protest against white racism. As played with controlled fury by James Earl Jones, the Jefferson character (based on Jack Johnson) dominates the screen. His one prolonged love scene with his white mistress is set up to serve as a plot-shift. They are in bed together when white policemen break into the room and arrest Jefferson for violation of the Mann Act. Since the film's focus is on Jefferson's frustration and anger, the audience is not required to be involved in his relationship to this girl, but rather in his hatred for white society. This is not an illegitimate device, but it does carefully avoid a serious probing of black-white romance.

The black ghetto school has been a topic that has had limited commercial success, but because it does not center on sex and violence, it does provide filmmakers with an opportunity to portray the emotions of Blacks with more authenticity. *Blackboard Jungle* was an early success. *Up the Down Staircase,* with Sandy Dennis as the harassed white teacher, was concerned with young Puerto Ricans in the ghetto and ended with a hopeful note. But *Halls of Anger,* a film whose setting is a Los Angeles black high school, represents a genuine breakthrough in depicting young black anger. It has no hopeful conclusion to the anger aroused when white students are bused in for superficial integration, but it permits a group of young black students to use ghetto lingo and display the frustration and hatred felt against a white-dominated school system.

Halls of Anger is an important film because it begins to approach a presentational — thus audience-involving — style. The film opens with a small group of white youngsters entering at the front of their new school through a hostile black gathering. Audience sympathy is not exclusively with white or black, though the only real film villain is a white tough who furnishes the plot-shift that brings on a school strike. Frustrated black youngsters resist the efforts of a black teacher to prepare them for a hostile society. The teacher touches on the inappropriateness of a white-oriented public school system in the black ghetto by tossing out traditional reading methods and giving his slow male readers sexy novels. There is also an excellent scene showing the black youngsters how much they actually know — though they know it in ghetto language — after a white student overwhelms them by his reading of English literary prose. The weakness of this film is in some of the scenes in which the action is stopped completely during a brief illustrated lecture on why things are the way they are. This is not so much the fault of the racial hangup as it is the result of a weakness in the film's script.

At least one American black-oriented film has made an honest effort to present artistically what it means to be black in a white culture. This is *Nothing But a Man*, a little-known, independently produced picture that, significantly enough, focuses entirely on a black man's movement from carefree bachelorhood to the restrictions and joys of married life. Ivan Dixon (the black POW in television's *Hogan's Heroes*) plays a railroad gang worker who stops over in a little Alabama community, where he meets, falls in love with, and marries the black school teacher (Abbey Lincoln). Their struggle to overcome background differences (he has a child by a former wife; she is an upper-class Black) is the core of the film. The Southern whites who do appear are peripheral, providing the oppressiveness against Dixon's desire to be "nothing but a man." But the picture is black-oriented, involving the audience — white and black — in identification in the re-creation of a life situation. As a "real" black family, the young couple provides audience involvement and presents the black man with his humanity. The picture, still popular in film societies, went nowhere commercially.

Gordon Parks, the famous still photographer, became the first black man to direct a major commercial picture (*Nothing But a Man* was directed by a white man), but unfortunately his *The Learning Tree* was no more than a well-intentioned illustration of growing up black. The view was sympathetic, but possibly Parks's inexperience as a director caused him to fall into a white-oriented style of moviemaking.

Melvin Van Peebles is another black director who seemed, at first, to have the same orientation. His first two films — *The Three-Day Pass* and *Watermelon Man* — were within the usual white-oriented framework, though dealing with racial subjects. His third film, however, is black-oriented, and has evoked squeals of pleasure from black audiences raised on white products. The picture is entitled *Sweet Sweetback's Baadasssss Song,* and it is a long cry of hostile frustration against white society. Dedicated to "black brothers and sisters who have had it with the Man," the picture turns the usual myths about black sexuality into the kind of reality black audiences can enjoy. White audiences are offended and frightened by the harsh vision Van Peebles projects, especially the obvious hatred expressed toward whites. The film is artistically uneven, but it does represent a new development in the commercial film aimed at a specifically black audience.

Future race films directed at white audiences may be stimulated into greater authenticity by works like *Sweetback.* Certainly their presence has made films that merely illustrate racial feelings more out of date than ever.

Chapter 4

CLINICAL, PSYCHOLOGICAL, AND LYRICAL

Sex in Cinema

Genres or types of films have come and gone in the history of cinema, depending on cultural interest. A current genre would be the motorcycle film, which reached its artistic peak in *Easy Rider*. Some genres, such as the Western and the musical, have maintained a fairly consistent interest to the American film public. But the most persistently popular genre remains the sex film, the picture that, in one way or another, concerns itself with the sexual attraction between male and female (or, in more recent fare, other groupings).

As recently as 1967, *A Guide for the Married Man* was considered by some to be advanced enough to represent a new breakthrough in screen frankness. In a *Christian Advocate* article in September of that year, I described that picture as part of a sex-comedy genre aimed at a general audience that wants to have its sexual kicks without guilt. This picture (made for the general audience rather than for the specialized audience of the "skin-flick" or nudie genre) was a natural development from the older Doris Day pictures, in which virtue was always preserved, but only after considerable suggestiveness that it might not be.

More recently, *Bob and Carol and Ted and Alice* appeared to be another breakthrough, but it, too, is in fact a direct descendant of the Day genre. Over the years the conventions of moral behavior have been stretched considerably, but the premise of a moral ending remains the same. In *BCTA* all the fun is in getting to the moral conclusion. The two couples finally reject the notion of mate-swapping, but only after the audience has been titilated by two hours of toying with the idea.

During the summer of 1970, two new films emerged to stretch the general conventions in the sex-film genre even further, pulling in for the mass audience elements that were previously limited to the specialized nudie-house trade. An examination of these two pictures will help us chart where we are at this moment in the evolution of the sex genre. We shall follow this with a critical evaluation of sexuality in film. The two films we shall consider are *Myra Breckinridge* and *Beyond the Valley of the Dolls,* both released by 20th Century Fox, apparently without regard for its reputation as a respectable business.

Myra Breckinridge has a peculiar cinematic ancestry. It has elements of black comedy, aligning it with a film far its superior, *M*A*S*H,* and with Tony Richardson's *The Loved One,* an older film that made fun of death and burial the way *M*A*S*H* makes fun of the games people play to avoid facing the reality of warfare. But *Myra Breckinridge* is more than a black comedy, it is also a polemic against Hollywood, a nasty, bitchy condemnation of the dream factory that fed the fantasies of America during the 1930s and 1940s.

Myra Breckinridge operates from the point of view that the superficial mass audience films of 1940-1950 created a sexual identity in American life that was covertly homosexual. Through the frequent use of clips from films of that period, Director Michael Sarne suggests that Hollywood emasculated the American male and celebrated homosexuality as the superior way of life. An example of the distortion Sarne resorts to in order to make his point is his use of clips from a Laurel and Hardy film that Fox released late in their careers to suggest that the arguments the boys had were fag battles.

Sarne's film is based on Gore Vidal's novel, itself a homosexual fantasy. This accounts in part for Sarne's preoccupation with homosexuality. But his dishonesty stems from the fact that his film clips are the work of the director, rather than the imagination of the film's central character (played by Raquel Welch). Vidal's book included references to old films in order to reflect Myra's preoccupation with Hollywood's version of reality. Since she is homosexual, this is the perspective projected. But in the film the clips do not come from Myra's imagination, but are inserted to ridicule the Hollywood imagery. All this is done with considerable distortion and dishonesty.

Sarne is interested only in talking *about* homosexuality, so he opens his film with the sexual surgery that converts Myron Breckinridge, homosexual, into Myra Breckinridge, beautiful female whose sole purpose in life is to seduce men and destroy their maleness through sodomy. Vidal's book does not reveal until the end that Myra was originally Myron, thus leading the reader into the homosexual fantasy without his knowledge, since he assumes he is seeing Hollywood and the world through the eyes of the beautiful and feminine Myra. By making Myra and Myron (played by film critic Rex Reed) coexist throughout the film, Sarne eliminates the artistic possibility that the audience will understand the homosexual fantasy from the inside. He is interested only in making a sex film with a male and female occupying the same body and exploiting the possibilities of this for dirty jokes.

Myra Breckinridge is a distasteful, vulgar motion picture. It has no specific nudity, no more strong language than usually found in mass audience films, and no sexual scenes of a conventional sort. In short, it contains no specific material that has in the past been censorable. Its fault lies in the theme chosen (homosexual rape and transvestism) and the manner in which this theme is treated (voyeuristically, rather than with insight).

Beyond the Valley of the Dolls made more money for Fox than did *Myra Breckinridge,* probably because it is concerned more with straight sex, including numerous scenes of female nudity. With this picture the skin flick has completed its evolution from seedy urban houses peopled by lonesome men to big city theaters and suburban houses visited by couples, both grey-haired and dating. Director Russ Meyer began as an independent filmmaker with a flair for turning male fantasies into modest money-makers. One of his earliest films was *The Immoral Mr. Teas,* in which a salesman fantasized that all the women up and down the street yearned to undress for him. Meyer's films have enjoyed considerable success because he lards them with a sense of humor and avoids the heavy-handed techniques of the sleazy pictures that try to be serious, sordid, and finally just moral enough to get past the "socially redemptive" requirement that keeps the vice squad at bay. He is an excellent film technician, a rarity in the skin-flick genre. His films are in sharp focus, have good color, and the actresses are good-looking girls who appear to enjoy their work. His biggest success was *Vixen,* a $700,000 picture that has grossed more than $6 million. In *Vixen* Meyer hangs together a slight story line about the wife of a north woods trapper who beds down with every male in sight, not to mention a lonesome female. The outdoor scenery was pleasant, an occasional fight enlivened the plot, and nudity abounded. *Vixen* played well in nudie houses, and in some cities it even had long runs in urban theaters. The Fox studios, which had spent as much as $10 million on some films to earn $8 million, decided to give Meyer what would be a big budget for him — more than $2 million.

Meanwhile, Fox was also considering ways of cashing in on another sex film, the enormously popular and crashingly dull *Valley of the Dolls,* based on Jacqueline Susann's novel of sex and drugs in Hollywood. Since Fox owned the rights to the title, the company decided to exploit it further and entitle Meyer's film *Beyond the Valley of the Dolls*. The picture bears no resemblance other than the title to the earlier picture. As a further guarantee of marketing success, the company allowed Meyer to hire an erudite young film critic, Roger Ebert of the Chicago *Sun-Times*, to write the script.

Beyond the Valley of the Dolls, however, is no *Vixen,* and it is nothing like the original *Valley.* Ebert wrote a script that put down the wooden formality of the earlier Meyer films, including all the phony plot devices he would laugh at as a critic. The villain in the piece is a Hamlet-like homosexual whose orgies make him the center of attention in the world of show business. Ebert's campy script takes up more time than is usually devoted to plot development in a Meyer film; as a result, the film appeals more to soap opera buffs than to devotees of the skin trade. There is nudity, of course, but not as much as there was in *Vixen.*

In addition to acquiring a bright script writer who ridicules him in his own picture, Meyer has also developed an interest in blood and gore. His last picture before *Beyond the Valley of the Dolls* was *Cherry, Harry and Raquel,* where the ending was excessively bloody. In *Beyond,* Meyer concludes his little sex outing with a decapitation, a sword stabbing, and two women gunned down, one with a pistol put into her mouth. This excess of blood changes the mood of a sex film. Possibly Meyer knows his audience well enough to figure out that they want "relevance" — ugly crimes committed by insane persons who then get their just reward.

In any event, Meyer has ceased to be a skin-flick maker and has become a purveyor of commercial trash for the middle classes. He has left one skin-flick subgenre — the straight nudie — and entered the world of the "relevant" exploration of the crucial problems facing contemporary society. At least that is the way the film appears on the surface. Whether Meyer realizes it or not, Ebert has given him a script that will have the sophisticated college students roaring with laughter. The girls in the film are naughty, but the really bad ones die, while the only slightly naughty ones end up marrying nice boys and living happily ever after.

Perhaps a new genre has been born, a picture that appeals on two levels to both segments, the left and the right. Presumably the sophisticates will recognize that *Beyond the Valley of the Dolls* is one long putdown on the mass-audience sex films, just as *Myra Breckinridge* is a homosexual interpretation of the 1940 Hollywood product. Meanwhile, the rest of the country will think it is seeing entertainment made possible by a permissive society. All of which suggests an image of a Fox executive with his left hand thumbing the nose and his right hand extended for the cash.

It would be naive to assume that negative reaction to *Myra Breckinridge* and *Beyond the Valley of the Dolls* will eliminate sexuality from American films. Because sex is an exceedingly important part of the human equation, and because films are commercial products, sex will continue in films.

Beyond the usual commercial and creative dimensions, however, sex in cinema has always raised social problems because of the uptightness about sex that prevails in our culture. Outrage greeted some of the earliest one-reelers already in 1896. In an article in *Chapbook,* a family periodical of the day, one writer responded to a film in this way:

> Now I want to smash the Vitascope. The name of the thing itself is a horror, but that may pass. Its manifestations are worse. The Vitascope, be it known, is a sort of magic lantern which reproduces movement. Whole scenes come and go, and the thing is mechanically ingenious, and a pretty toy for that great child, the public. Its managers are not satisfied with this,

however, and they bravely set out to eclipse in vulgarity all previous theatrical attempts.

In a recent play called "The Widow Jones" you may remember a famous kiss which Miss May Irwin bestowed on a certain John C. Rise and vice versa. Neither participant is physically attractive, and the spectacle of their prolonged posturing on each other's lips was hard to bear. When only life-size, it was pronounced beastly. But that was nothing to the present sight. Magnified to gargantuan proportions and peated three times over, it is absolutely disgusting. . . . The Irwin Kiss is no more than a lyric of the stockyards. Such things call for police interference.

The response of that nineteenth-century writer to a simple kiss was relative to the mores of his day. An increasing number of critics today are expressing outrage over sexual explicitness in films. These are not only religious or pietistic critics. Judith Crist, describing *Spencer's Mountain*, scored it for its "smirking sexuality." Billed as a "wholesome" film, *Spencer's Mountain* was in fact a commercial exploitation of public interest in sex, placed within a story that is "cheap, tasteless and patronizing."*

But this film that offended Miss Crist might have struck other viewers as an uplifting story of a boy who wants to go to college. Are these different reactions simply another case of what is in the eye of the beholder? I think not. Rather, it is a case of a confusion of critical methodology. The discursive-presentational structure we discussed in Chapter Two can be applied to films that deal with sexuality. We can adapt the terms somewhat to make the application pertinent to the experience of viewing such films. The mode of perception primarily located at the presentational end of the viewing continuum is somewhat akin to an *artistic* experience of sex. The mode closer to the discursive end is *voyeuristic,* a seeing without involvement at any significant level.

There is danger in using the term "artistic" because of the many connotations "art" has, but I shall try to make

The Private Eye, the Cowboy, and the Very Naked Girl (Holt, Rinehart, Winston, 1968), p. 5.

explicit how I am using the term in this context. An artistically effective use of sexuality in film will place sex in a proper context and present it to the audience in such manner that the audience becomes involved. The difference between the voyeuristic experience and the artistic experience is the difference between the film that merely illustrates and the film that involves. The voyeuristic film may satisfy someone's curiosity, but at the same time, it degrades sexuality by separating it from its proper context. This distinction between the audio-visual, noninvolving film and the presentational, involving film experience is very important. I do not mean to imply that the male audience — and to a certain extent the female audience — would not be involved in a voyeuristic sex film. But this would be spectator involvement, resulting from curiosity or self-centered titillation. The artistic experience, on the other hand, breaks open reality in such a manner that we may be led to a new understanding of sexuality.

In this connection I find it helpful to consider styles of film-making in three categories that deal with sex: *clinical, psychological, or lyrical.* I will expand on these categories with the understanding that they inevitably overlap within the same film. As in the case of my overall methodology dealing with modes of perception — discursive-presentational — these categories are designed to provide handles with which to grasp something of the complexity of film.

Hans Richter, the German avant-garde artist and noted filmmaker, insists on a distinction between the film that records reality and the film that creates a new reality. According to Richter, "the free use of cinematic expression" enables the filmmaker to take the object out of its conventional context and put it into new relationships, creating in that way a new content altogether."* For Richter this has meant showing persons or objects in such

*Quoted in Lawson, *Film: The Creative Process* (Hill and Wang, 1964), p. 223.

a way that they no longer conform to our normal visual experience. In his film *Dreams Money Can Buy,* for example, based on a collage by Max Ernest, Richter superimposes, plays with time, and edits in order to deal with the vision of the absurd that he feels accurately reflects the contemporary situation.

His insistence, however, that film is most effective when it permits us to see more than the normal visual experience helps us to see the difference between the stag film and the sensual film. One shows the clinical reality in front of the camera; the other shows the full meaning of that reality and suggests its significance for the viewer. One is an audio-visual aid; the other the presentation of an experience.

The Legion of Decency and the Hays Office of the 1930s and 1940s forced Hollywood to handle sexuality through devious tricks. The end result of this was the cycle of Doris Day films that built on the classic dramatic technique that the audience knew something that the heroine did not know — whether or not she had had intercourse with the leading man while she was intoxicated. This technique of enjoying immorality so long as the ending is moral was, in fact, created by the restrictions of the Legion and the Hays office. Sexuality thus became disguised.

Not all treatment of sexuality in film during this period bore the marks of these restrictions. Some films did display an artistic vision of sex. Jean Renoir, the son of painter Auguste Renoir, made films that celebrated the sad happiness of sexual desire. *A Day in the Country* was one of the first. It bears the stylishness of its day — the coy female, the roguish men bent on seduction, and the stupid husband easily deceived. But within the context of this style, which seems a bit dated now, the handling of sexuality enables us to recognize that clinical material is not essential to the artistic presentation of sensuality.

Renoir places his performers within the ecology of nature. He celebrates all that lives, lovingly examining the countryside in which human sensuality pulsates. (A recent example of this merging of nature and sexuality is found in the film version of D. H. Lawrence's *Women in Love,* where the hero races nude through the grain field and caresses the foliage sensually in a manner repeated a few moments later with a young blonde girl hardly distinguished from the golden beauty of the field itself. Lawrence's vision of sexuality tends to be too cerebral and self-centered for my taste, but the fact remains that he was urging us to accept sexuality as an integral part of all that is, and the film version successfully conveys this.)

Renoir sets up a situation of potential sensuality by pairing off two racy young men with the flighty mother and her shy, virginal daughter. He builds on the tension inherent in such a situation, and he resolves it in a manner that indicates he is aware that coitus is but a fraction of the total love experience. His film is heavy with sensuality and symbolism, but it is intended as a story depicting real persons engaged in real experiences. It engages the viewer because it presents the experience in such a way that he is not merely observing the encounter between a man and a woman, but is himself drawn into the experience. Obviously not every viewer will be so involved, but the intent is nonetheless one of personal involvement, just as Beethoven's symphonies are presented to involve the hearer in a musical experience and not merely to record tones, sounds, and rhythm.

We can refer to this kind of artistic presentational film in terms of what it actually says about its subject as well as the effect it has on the viewer involved in the experience. This we do because we are dealing with a story about two couples and a deceived husband. In such a cinematic presensation there is a plot, and the plot is not without significance. But what really matters is the vision of the artist and the way his vision draws the viewer into the experience he wishes to share.

Other films that involve, rather than merely illustrate, may depend even less on plot. The commercial theater has been reluctant to use many films of this sort, but the avant-garde movement has devoted itself almost exclusively to the nonplot film. Richter says that the film artist must revolt against "realism" because

> Problems of modern art lead directly into film. Organizations and orchestration of form, color, the dynamics of motion, simultaneity, were problems with which Cézanne, the cubists, and the futurists had to deal. The connection to theater, and literature, was completely severed.*

Little known to filmgoers who restrict themselves to commercial theaters, the avant-garde movement has placed heavy emphasis on the presentation of sensual material, dealing with it in symbols and rhythms and evoking in the viewer an awareness of the depths of sensuality with a minimum of concern with literal material. Unfortunately, the avant-garde material that gets the most publicity is that which shows actual physical intercourse, but rarely is this done by genuine avant-garde film artists except to suggest the lyrical nature of physical union or to caricature the modern preoccupation with sex.

An early example of a highly symbolic, avant-garde film dealing with sensuality was *The Clergyman and the Seashell*, an experimental film of the 1920s. Plot is virtually lost in this film. In its place is a heavy concentration on symbolism, especially Freudian symbolism. The filmmaker tried to create a new reality rather than simply record reality. His effort was not to disguise sexuality but to point to the larger meaning behind sexual feelings. With its heavy debt to avant-garde painting and to Freudianism, *The Clergyman and the Seashell* seems dated, but its value lies in the way it tries to deal symbolically, rather than literally, with sensual material. Its treatment of sexuality is

*Quoted in Lawson, *op. cit.*, p. 223.

not clinical, but neither is it lyrical. It uses *psychological* symbolism.

Another film that is somewhat dated, but much better known because of its historic fight over censorship, is Hedy Lamar's *Ecstasy*. Because it included a brief sequence depicting a nude girl, the picture was banned in this country and released only after a long court fight. To see it today is to be sharply reminded of how mores have changed, for what is actually shown in this film clinically or literally would justify little more than a GP rating by today's standards. The sexuality of *Ecstasy* is of the lyrical variety in that it seeks to evoke in the viewer an awareness of deep longing and passion. It presents sexuality in a purely subjective mood, and also utilizes symbolism (bees, flowers, horses) in a rather obvious way.

One of the sequences in *Ecstasy* that created censorship problems showed the young girl swimming in a lake, losing her clothes, chasing her horse across the field (the camera almost always at a discreet distance), and finally facing a young man who rescues her horse and her clothes. The girl is a young bride who has left her husband, an older man, because he has chosen not to consummate their marriage. After the meeting in the field with the young man, the girl returns to her father's home and broods over her need for the man. A highly stylized sequence follows, in which she leaves her bedroom, plays the piano for a few minutes, and finally decides to seek out the man for romance. The scene in the man's little cabin is — again by today's standards — clinically mild; but within its style it is an interesting attempt to create a lyrical mood of passion finally fulfilled. The remainder of *Ecstasy* is slow-moving narrative in which the rejected husband shoots himself. The camera extends his fall to the floor and death with several different angle shots. The final few frames are a montage of the young man at work building a bridge.

The lake and cabin sequences disturbed the American

public. But if we agree that, in the tripartite division of clinical, psychological, and lyrical, *Ecstasy* is predominantly a lyrical film, why was it so disturbing? Simply because people saw it entirely on the clinical level. Objections were raised to the nudity and the passion expressed in Hedy Lamar's face during what was apparently an intercourse scene, though this is by no means explicit.

What are the values in treating sexuality from any one of these three vantage points? The clinical, in varying degrees, is an audio-visual experience; the psychological is concerned with symbolically describing sexual feelings as with the interpersonal relationship involved in sexuality; the lyrical is concerned with the subjective rendering of a feeling regarding sexuality. These three areas are in fact interwoven to such a degree that it is seldom possible to find one without at least some element of the other two. In general, however, one of the three dominates.

I am suggesting that one method of critically evaluating sexuality in film is to determine which of these three categories predominates in the material, how effectively it is done, and what purpose it serves. *A Day in the Country,* for example, is largely lyrical, using a natural setting, a trivial plot, and a moment of discreet kissing to create a sensual mood. *Ecstasy,* too, is largely lyrical, but it depends a bit more on clinical data for establishing its lyrical mood.

To look at a more recent film, Robert Altman's *M*A*S*H* utilizes sexual material for purposes other than sex. This film deals with the absurdity of man's killing man, and it deliberately offends the myths by which we live in order to expose their inadequacy. Opinion differs as to how effective this exposure is. The point is that just as religion is ridiculed not to attack God but to attack the Army major's rigid exploitation of religion as a means of avoiding any true relationship to life, the major's sexual encounter with Hot Lips is ridiculed in order to expose the two of them as inauthentic moralists. There is finally so much cruelty to Hot Lips' treatment, especially in her shower scene, that the sequence loses its effectiveness, but its intent is to use sex as an instrument of ridicule.

Sexuality involves human relationships that include the dimension of physical contact. This experience creates a sense of oneness with another; it includes a physiological response; and it carries with it a certain degree of responsibility to the larger community. The ingredients to this mix of sexuality include the glance, the smile, the perfume, the music, the physical body, and ultimately, though not essentially, coitus. *M*A*S*H,* however, uses clinical sex for other purposes. It does not pretend to create a sense of oneness with another; it will not create a physiological response; and it makes no effort to deal with the meaning of sex in the larger context of community responsibility. In this sense sex is not the focus of *M*A*S*H;* it is merely an instrument to another end. The film must therefore be judged on the effectiveness of its use of religion, sex, Army life, and revolt against authority, in carrying out its larger purpose, that is, its attack on false values and its celebration of the value of freedom.

My Night with Maud is another film that uses sexual desire to deal with human relationships. There is absolutely no clinical material in this film. Its focus is the feeling a man has for two women and the conflict he has with himself as he seeks to choose between them. It is, in one sense, a *cinema verite* film (fiction, of course, like *Faces*) that includes some extremely perceptive insights into human sexuality. But the important thing about *My Night with Maud* is that its focus is on relationships and commitment. It is psychological, but it is not so much symbolic as interpersonal.

Our reaction to sexual material in film is influenced by whether we approach a film as a social document or look at it aesthetically. We can never do one without the other;

but one of the two will be dominant, and this will strongly affect our reaction to the film.

Of the three categories — clinical, psychological, lyrical — clinical material creates the greatest problem in America because the explicit depiction of sexual conduct is so threatening to the public psyche. According to popular American mythology, the sight of a bare female breast is supposed to stimulate the male viewer to conduct unbecoming his moral standards. Another related objection to nudity is the idea that it is necessary to keep covered the private aspects of human sexuality. Our culture has, over the centuries, decreed that certain human activity is of such a nature that it should remain hidden from public view.

The question of why sexual material is so threatening to the American public is a very complex one, and we cannot possibly cover all facets of the topic. But it will be helpful to examine a small part of it. We might begin with the view of sexuality that has prevailed in much Roman Catholic and Protestant theology: the idea that sex is for procreation only, and that any sexual activity not directed at the propagation of the race is wrong. Thus, in Roman Catholic practice, birth control is forbidden on the grounds that a natural function of sex — procreation — is blocked. Extending this principle, any sexual stimulus that does not have as its ultimate goal the procreation of children is wrong. A man may see his wife's unclothed body, because in practice this stimulus can lead to intercourse, which could lead to the birth of children. The same man may not see the unclothed body of a strange woman — especially his neighbor's — for he will surely covet that form.

The trouble with this simplistic understanding of sexual stimulus is that it ignores the reality that loving the world involves cherishing and celebrating the world. Thus, a nude form may indeed serve as a stimulus to lust, but it may also enhance humanity. We must conclude, therefore, that it is not the fact of nudity or sexual behavior that appeals to selfish lust, but the manner of treatment.

The act of sexual intercourse itself is so freighted with mental baggage that I find it difficult to imagine a depiction of the sexual act that is artistically essential to a film. Yet in a well-known Danish film of several years ago, *A Stranger Knocks*, the act of intercourse was essential to the plot because the woman involved noticed a tattoo on her lover's arm that identified him as her husband's killer. This discovery came in the midst of the physical act of union, and turned her cries of ecstasy into shouts of horror. The intercourse here, however, was suggested rather than shown. The event of intercourse was essential to the point of the plot. It could happen again, and the need for physical appearance of the act could also happen. Still, the nature of the sexual act is such that its clinical depiction tends to be somewhat awkward and perhaps a bit silly.

I submit that it is possible to deal with nudity and sexuality in one of two ways: either to celebrate humanity or denigrate it. And this is the criterion I would place on its use. The famous bare breast scene in *The Pawnbroker* was dramatically important — whether or not it was essential could be debated — in that it triggered the pawnbroker into memories that he had tried to suppress. The closing scenes of *The Killing of Sister George*, on the other hand, are clinically revealing, but they are excessive relative to the point of the remainder of the material in the film and therefore overbalanced in a way that degrades sexuality rather than enhancing it.

There is a bedroom scene in *La Guerre Est Finie* that succeeds because it fits appropriately into the artistic vision of Director Alain Renais. The camera caresses the feminine form of Ingrid Thulin, who is with her lover (Yves Montand). The nudity is casual, not studied or deliberate. The camera glances, it does not stare. The concern is obviously with the relationship between these two people, and the recognition that this sexual embrace is an important part of that relationship is apparent. On a less sophisticated level, the bedroom encounter in *A Man and a Woman* fits the total film and is designed to convey a part of the larger whole, not simply to exploit the sexual experience itself.

These examples, however, deal with sexuality as a part of the larger complex of human relationships. What are we to say regarding a film that is devoted exclusively to erotic material? To what extent is this a legitimate enterprise? I know of one study center on sexuality that has produced its own film of intercourse, a lyrical, but also very definitely clinical, portrayal of a couple — in this case a married couple. Judging such a film on aesthetic grounds, we would ask that it be authentic to the experience itself; that it portray this relationship with respect for the event itself; and that it celebrate humanity rather than denigrate it. Is it possible to do this successfully? I suspect that it is, but my own aesthetic judgment is faulty, because I am a child of an environment that has surrounded this event with such awe that I suspect I could not render a positive judgment on the aesthetic value of this film. No doubt a viewer twenty years younger than I, who grew up in a different culture, would approach such a film differently.

Socially, of course, there are additional considerations. A married couple watching such a film might react in a way that enhanced their own marriage. But what of the 14 year-old youngster? Is this too massive a stimulus for him or her at this age? This is a family and a social question. I would be inclined to think it would be excessive, though I confess that I would prefer such a child to see a lyrical rather than a purely clinical film, so that at least some of the additional dimensions of the physical act would be apparent to him.

Beyond the aesthetic and social questions is a moral one. Here I would insist that we put the moral question to the filmmaker and the exhibitor. A film itself is not immoral. Only the action of the team that develops the film could be said to be immoral, if we mean by "immoral" the willful violation of standards to the detriment of oneself and others. Part of the moral question, then, is: What is the vision of the filmmaker and how effectively is he conveying that vision? This will be a subjective judgment, but if in the opinion of the viewer a film intends to celebrate sexuality, and if the film's purpose is realized, then the filmmaker is not immoral. If, on the other hand, there is deliberate exploitation of the topic, an inauthentic rendering of sexuality, and false values proffered about sexuality, then there is immorality. Each film must be judged in its own context and each viewer must make his own judgment. *Ecstasy* is certainly a well-intended film by today's standards. It may have been considered exploitative in its day, but the showing of it today could hardly be considered denigrative to humanity.

What we have done in this chapter is to examine film as an art form that exists in a social context. We have considered the sexual content of film from the aesthetic and social dimensions. In developing our sensitivities to this sexuality, we have made a distinction between those films that are merely voyeuristic and those that are artistically involving. We have suggested that the actual treatment of sexual material in a film might concentrate on one of three forms: the clinical, the psychological, and the lyrical. At times (as in *M*A*S*H* or Fellini's *Satyricon*) one of these forms might be used to illustrate something other than sex. At other times, one of these forms may be presented for specifically erotic purposes. Whether this is good or bad must be judged in terms of whether sexuality is presented in a manner that enhances or denigrates sex. The appropriateness of a film presentation of sexuality will vary in different generations; it is a matter essentially culturally conditioned.

Sex and art go together. They have been friends for generations. Sex and exploitation have also spent time together. Our task is to encourage the first relationship and discourage the second.

Chapter 5

ALTERNATIVES TO REPRESSION

The Question of Censorship

It is reasonable to expect that films will become more explicit in the future, showing scenes of intimacy that were not even discussed in the privacy of homes several years ago. We may not like to see this increased exposure, but in our pluralistic society it appears to be inevitable.

Operating within the framework proposed in this book, I am well aware that the presentational vision of a film can have a great impact on the emotional make-up of a viewer. Because younger viewers are more susceptible to such molding, I have a particular concern for the quality of films they see. A utopian society would guarantee emotional experiences for children appropriate to their age-level, but in this pluralistic society, lacking even a definition of such appropriateness, this is hardly possible. The report of the President's Commission on Obscenity included some minority recommendations that all restrictions on obscenity be removed on the ground that there is no evidence that such material is in fact harmful to the average child. For a generation schooled to believe that the "obscene" — however defined — is harmful to the young, such a proposal sounds far too radical. But somewhere down the line, I suspect, this will be adopted. I am convinced that obscenity is entirely a matter of taste, and taste will always vary from culture to culture and from subculture to subculture.

Meanwhile, we live in a pluralistic society composed of a few libertarians, a somewhat larger number of strict puritans, and the majority of the nation with mixed emotions in between. At this moment in history, I suggest that the much-maligned motion picture rating system is the best stopgap measure for protecting the sensibilities of the young and the freedom of the rest of us.

In this chapter I want to look briefly at that system, which is administered by the Motion Picture Association of America (MPAA). Before doing so, we shall take a brief look at the kind of forces that go into a society and make a rating system necessary.

Several decades ago Sigmund Freud articulated the thesis that Western civilization is the product of repression, man's ego gaining control over his id, with the strong moral guidance of his superego. For Freud, repression *per se* is not evil; it is the control that man and his society establish in order to hold in check those forces that otherwise might run amok and create chaos.

Against this background of civilization-as-repression (which is not the entire story by any means), the individual in a democracy is offered a freedom to realize his fullest potential. The tension between these two positions is the tension of a free man living in a society that has the right to establish certain restrictions in order to provide for the larger good. Value-protector forces — churches, schools, self-appointed censors — have assumed the role of determining those restrictions, based on certain presuppositions as to what is of value to man and society.

Aligned against the value-protector forces have been creative and economic forces, one wanting to express itself freely, the other wanting to sell a product. The motion picture industry is an example of this combination of creativity with commerce, a combination that places the defender of creativity in camp with the defender of commercial exploitation. These opposing forces, with vastly differing motives, have spent the last seventy years trying to reconcile the freedom to view and the right to control. The dialogue that has taken place is itself a short history of American culture, with touches of religious bigotry, shameful exploitation, and joyous creativity. To trace this history, it should be helpful to examine what French film critic Andre Bazin has called cinema's "geographic river profile."

Bazin notes that a river will maintain a certain direction for a time, but then, for reasons that are clear only in part, it will change directions and its profile will never again be the same. Cinema has done this, changing directions at certain points in its history, due in part to social changes, in part to the creative efforts of one or more filmmakers, and in part to forces that will not hold still for clear cultural analysis.

Film artists emerge and make an impact on the river's profile. Orson Welles appeared on the scene in 1941 and made *Citizen Kane*. The techniques he used and the way he used them, forming them into a cinematic whole, resulted in a film that was of such significance that all pictures made since are in some way indebted to Welles. Once a man like Welles appears, the cinema river profile is never again the same. Another direction has been assumed, at times changing the profile only slightly, at other times drastically.

These changes come in various forms. John Huston's *Battle of San Pietro* was a breakthrough in authentic filmmaking about war. The United States government promptly banned the picture, withdrawing it from distribution. Sections were deleted and the picture was doctored up by the addition of a solemn prologue by General Mark Clark, praising the brave men who fought in the battle about to be seen. What Huston did was to follow an American unit into battle in Italy, carefully depicting what the grubby struggle for hills and valleys was all about. San Pietro was not terribly important and its capture may or may not have had an impact on the war. But men died there, and it is this dying that Huston shares, raising the deeper question of the absurdity of all wars.

A film questioning the war in 1945 was too strong. Films on war in 1970 cannot possibly do anything but question war. What is the difference? The cultural climate has changed, the river profile has changed — partly because of films like *San Pietro,* more so because of cultural patterns, and still more so because of certain dimensions of life now available to rational explanation.

In Freudian terminology health is determined by the ego's awareness of his superego's identity, but not by his elimination of the superego. Self-awareness means knowing what repressive forces are at work and judging them accordingly. Awareness of what an individual and his society repress is important to the mental health of an individual and his society. It is this awareness that enables individuals and society to function to their fullest potential.

Through this century, as the value-protector forces have clashed with the creative (and economic) forces, crucial moments have occurred in the cinema river profile that reflect society's inability to recognize that creative forces were pushing forward toward a new potential for man. Instead of accepting this surge forward as something of value for man's ongoing development, the value-protectors have seen it as a threat to his existence, and they have reacted with repression.

Examination of the films that have caused censorship problems in the past few decades will illustrate the dangers of this repression. In 1919, Eric von Stroheim directed *Blind Husbands,* a moody film depicting the temptation that befell a wealthy American lady confronted by a sophisticated European count. Her dull husband was blind to her emotional needs. By today's standards, this kind of flirtation (and it never gets past this stage) is mild indeed, but in 1919, public unease about Von Stroheim's work was strong. The reason: he was revealing something about women that the American public did not want to face, that is, that women have desires as strongly as men do. This equality in sexuality was related, in part, to the general rise in feminism, and it had been heightened by World War I, when women had to go to work in industry. Von Stroheim was simply portraying in fictional form something about women that repressive forces feared.

Through the 1920s, film titles and subjects grew more involved in sex. Very little explicit nudity or sexual behavior was shown, but much was suggested, discursively illustrating the jazz-age freedom that was threatening to the repressive value-protectors. It was in this era that the Hays Office was born, created by the film industry to offset the strong criticism that arose after several scandals involving Hollywood stars and an increased number of "sexy" film titles.

Mae West personified sex in the early 1930s, but she was only bringing to the screen the risqué suggestiveness of the burlesque stage. *She Done Him Wrong,* made with Cary Grant in 1933, was filled with double entendres delivered with Mae West's slow drawl that successfully made fun of sex. But this picture, mild by today's standards, so incensed many Roman Catholics that it is credited with an assist in bringing the Legion of Decency into existence. And all her subsequent films were so toned down that she quickly lost her edge and her box office power.

In retrospect such films as *Blind Husbands* and *She Done Him Wrong* could hardly have damaged the public psyche in their day, but to say this is to speak from the perspective of the 1970's. It might be argued that they were detrimental, adding to a slow erosion of morality in the country. But could this have been proved at the time? Can we be certain of it now? Research may some day be helpful to us in this connection, but for the time being, the question is a purely speculative one.

Repression does take place when the value-protectors of society prevail over the creative artist or the commercial interests. When is such repression valuable and when is it a danger? There is no clear answer, but it is certain that the best way to get at the answer is to have the fullest possible awareness of what is behind the repressiveness.

The *Christian Advocate* once printed a photograph of black militant James Forman on its cover. The picture was repeated three times on the inside of the magazine as an editorial tie, suggesting that the story ran over several pages. Much of the reaction to the magazine's editorial treatment of the Black Manifesto centered on the use and repetition of this picture. The editorial purpose was clear: emphasis on but not endorsement of Forman. Yet many intelligent readers were infuriated that Forman's picture stared at them from four pages in one issue of the magazine.

These readers were exhibiting what I would call the censor mentality" — the desire to repress something without knowing what it is that one wants to repress. The letter-writers and callers were not angry with the *Advocate* — they were angry with Forman and the church leaders who had given him a hearing. But they attacked the *Advocate* because it was a handy vehicle for attack. Because the magazine printed the picture, it was wrong. Its editor should have been fired or the magazine done away with altogether.

This is the censor-mentality at work. Anger at Forman's stance and even strong disagreement with him and his demands is understandable. But to want to stop his picture from having appeared on the cover of a church magazine was to react against the wrong target. Censoring the *Advocate* obviously would not stop Forman, but in their frustration some readers somehow thought that it would be at least a first step.

Are there times when the shift in the cinema river profile is not in the best interests of all of society? There may be. But any attempt to identify such an occasion must be made with the utmost care. Blocking changes in the profile is a heavy responsibility in a society that places such high premium on freedom. What is essential is for society to be aware of why it feels the need to repress. I suspect the best alternative is to allow maximum freedom for adults and minimum freedom for the young. But by "young" it is no longer possible to mean teen-agers. Here I am actually referring to the preteen, that youngster who, because of his pre-puberty make-up, is not yet concerned with the problems of adolescence and consequently need not, and should not, be exposed to information and emotional film data that might distort his image of sexuality and other areas that concern society.

There is no final solution; there is only a process toward the resolution of the tension between creativity and repression. I prefer to opt for the side of creativity because it is not at all clear to me that artistic (and/or commercial) material is *that* harmful to the young and the adult. In spite of what censorship forces tell us, there is no evidence that obscene material "poisons" the mind. It may not help, and it may anesthetize, but I am not yet convinced that it poisons.

Lacking certainty on this score, we can only live with the tension between the two opposing forces. The cinema river profile must be granted maximum freedom to shift direction. At times, to push the analogy, it will be destructive to the crops along the river bank, but at other times, it will go deeper and in much more creative directions.

I have supported, endorsed, and encouraged the motion picture rating system because I see it as a limited but effective means of permitting the cinema river profile to continue to develop. In this support I have stood with the National Council of Churches and the National Catholic

Office for Motion Pictures in advising and criticizing the system since it began in November 1968. The rating system seems to be a practical way of protecting the buying public — especially the young — and at the same time providing the film artist (in his commercial setting) freedom to be at his creative best.

Who can we rely upon to classify films in advance? In some instances, the federal government has standards that it enforces through agencies such as the Food and Drug Administration. But food and drugs are a different kind of commodity from the film, which is a creative art form produced and distributed through a commercial outlet. Because it is a creative art form, standards are almost impossible to set. Therefore, self-regulation by the industry itself seems to me to be the most reasonable method of classifying films.

The rating system is in existence because we do not live in a perfect society. The filmmakers in a perfect society would be concerned only to produce creative works of art that would have a beneficial effect on the viewer (and in such a perfect society they would, presumably, know what was really beneficial). The parents in such a society would be concerned with their children's well-being and know them well enough to make an accurate determination of which films were suitable for them to see.

Such a perfect society obviously does not exist. Ours is a free society, and freedom is a dangerous thing. Dependency is secure. We place ourselves under the control of another person or of a large company or of the government, because here we find security from the uncertain and the unknown. But freedom is a risk. We do not know what tomorrow brings, but we know that our own decisions must be made as we face each new situation.

A free society takes risks. It permits free behavior in order to guarantee maximum creativity and decision-making among its people. That this is an imperfect society is shown by the fact that filmmakers take advantage of this freedom to exploit the buying public, and that parents are irresponsible in the way they raise and guide their children.

The MPAA rating system is basically an information service, an indication by the film industry itself that tells the audience what the industry feels is the age suitability of each particular film. No one, of course, including the film rating office, operates without prior criteria. Its rating decisions reflect what it feels to be suitable for certain ages. You and I might make different ratings, but this is the industry — acting collectively — making its judgment.

Since November 1, 1968, all American films have been rated with one of four ratings: G — General audiences; GP — Mature audiences; anyone may attend, but parents are advised that the film may contain material that they prefer their children to avoid; R — Restricted; theater owners agree to admit no one under 17 (or, in some areas, 18) unless he is accompanied by a parent or adult guardian; X — no one under 17 (or 18) is admitted.

The advertising for each film carries the rating, and theater owners agree to carry out the rating at the box office. This system is geared to advise parents as to the suitability of films for children. It does not attempt to make artistic judgments regarding films, only to inform of their suitability for children.

By mid-1971 there had been 1243 films rated by the MPAA rating office. Of that number only 89 were given an X rating. (This figure does not include those exploitation films which self-apply the X for their own promotional purposes.) The X rating marks a film that is released by a company but does not possess the MPAA's Code Seal of Approval. In other words, MPAA is saying that if a film is rated X the industry feels that it fails to meet its standards of quality and it is therefore not considered of value even for adults.

This does not prohibit filmmakers from making, nor

distributors from distributing, nor theater owners from exhibiting, X films. They are free to do so, but the product itself has been duly labeled as to content.

What are the alternatives to ratings? The United States has never had a national censorship law, but many states and communities have had local laws and ordinances to control the viewing of film. These have gradually disappeared because of various rulings by the Supreme Court, which have granted films the protection of the First Amendment (freedom of speech).

This has not always been the case. A 1913 decision of the Court *(Mutual Film Corporation v. the Industrial Commission of Ohio)* said that film does not fall under the First Amendment. The State of Ohio was demanding the right to see all films prior to their release. Mutual Film Corporation, a distributor of films, claimed this as a violation of the First Amendment. The Court said, in 1913:

> The exhibition of moving pictures is a business pure and simple, originated and conducted for profit, like other spectacles, not to be regarded, nor intended to be regarded by the Ohio Constitution, we think, as part of the press of the country, or as organs of public opinion. They are mere representations of facts. . . .

This opinion was changed in 1948 in a case involving Paramount Pictures. In the same case the movie industry was declared to be in violation of the Sherman Antitrust Act and had to divest itself of monopolistic holdings of both producing and theater outlets. The companies were allowed to produce and distribute, but not to hold exclusive rights to exhibit. In the 1948 opinion, the Court said:

> We have no doubt that moving pictures, like newspapers and radio, are included in the press whose freedom is guaranteed by the First Amendment.

Once it had this protection, the only barrier to filmmaking remained the obscenity laws, for obscenity, however defined, is not protected by the First Amendment as currently interpreted.

A long history of obscenity cases reached a climax in the 1957 case of *Roth v. the U.S.*, where the statement was made that the only test for obscenity was "whether to the *average* person, applying contemporary community standards, the *dominant* theme of the material *taken as a whole* appeals to prurient interest" (italics mine). If a film fails to meet this standard, it can be declared obscene, and is therefore not protected by the First Amendment.

The Court ruled in 1961 that a community or state may not hold up the showing of a film for an unduly long time in order to classify it — no more than three days — for this becomes prior restraint. A film may be shown, and then if it is felt to be obscene, the local authorities may bring suit against it as violating the obscenity laws, which operate under the standards set forth in *Roth v. the U.S.*

More recently, in a Dallas, Texas, case, the Court shifted its position on the First Amendment, and said, in effect, that this particular freedom does not apply to minors. This came in connection with a ruling disallowing a case brought up from a lower court upholding a Dallas classification system. Local authorities had established a classification system and placed the film *Viva Marie* in the adult category. The film company fought back, and in ruling for the film company, the Court said, in effect, communities *may* restrict the showing of films to minors, but not to adults.

The classification system came into effect shortly thereafter, in an effort to have the industry provide this classification rather than rely on the uncertainty of each local community. And this is what it, in fact, does. Each film is labeled for adult or general consumption. It is then up to the local theater manager to publicize and enforce this label.

Chapter 6

FILM CRITICISM

Some Examples

Within a pluralistic culture a rating system established by filmmakers themselves is at best a stopgap measure to inform and assist the public. To provide creative input beyond such a system, informed viewers are necessary, a public that has a taste that responds to films of value and rejects films that demean and distort humanity.

We need a public of "film critics" — not professionals, of course, but discriminating viewers who make judgments against and for films based on sound cinematic principles. In developing the methodology discussed in this book I have sought to provide a framework within which such critical evaluations can be made. Certain tools have been suggested. These are only methods. The individual must render his own judgment on the films he sees or ignores.

In this final chapter several reviews are printed. They appear here as they first appeared in the *Christian Advocate*. All of them represent one critic's immediate reaction to particular films. They are written out of the presentational-discursive methodology, which will be more apparent in some reviews than in others. I trust they will serve as a stimulus, not so much for the writing of criticism — though that too is badly needed — but for the personal criticism each of us must bring to his filmgoing experience. For it is finally the filmgoing public that says yes to the truly creative changes in the cinema river profile.

John F. Kennedy: Years of Lightning, Day of Drums
(Embassy)
Produced by George Stevens, Jr.; directed by Bruce
Herschenson; screenplay by Bruce Herschenson; narrated
by Gregory Peck.

The incomprehensible, brutal, and senseless murder of
President John F. Kennedy is recreated in this moving account of that "day of drums" when the entire world
grieved, set against the background of those "years of
lightning" when a new political style of life blessed us by
its presence.

Originally made by the United States Information
Agency for overseas distribution only, the picture was so
well received that Congress made a special exception and
permitted its domestic distribution. Because several years
have passed since that black November weekend in 1963,
it is possible to view these scenes with some of the detach-
ment that time provides. I would not have wanted to experience it any sooner, since, as Gregory Peck notes in his
narration, John Kennedy's death was an unexpected,
shocking reminder that "no man can control that string of
time that is his life."

Yet even now it is an emotional shock to see the President first come on the screen, moving with quiet dignity
through crowds toward the inaugural platform. It is sheer
torment to experience his joy while knowing how short is
his time among us. Cutting from the funeral procession
back to Kennedy's accomplishments, the film underscores
the theme of a full life, the happy, creative, successful life,
but the viewer is sobered by an awareness that Kennedy's
presidency will last for only two years and ten months.

One wonders whether future generations will understand how much Kennedy meant to us. He gave his generation a style that demanded the freedom to love life under
the iron discipline of achieving the task at hand. In retro-

spect, it now seems that he was almost unreal, too handsome, too strong, too firm and resolute in the face of Russian threats, space disappointments, and threats of world hunger. We had no right to expect him to combine the wit and intellect of Stevenson with the political sagacity of Roosevelt. But after eight years of the Eisenhower status quo, Kennedy's vigor, phrase-making, and honesty charged us with excitement; and we began to believe that leadership had indeed passed to a new generation and that progress over insurmountable problems was a possibility. He made it sound so right to say that since "wars are created by man, they can be ended by man."

Then he was snatched away by forces of ignorance and a twisted mentality, moving to a pinpoint of history that sums up the absurdity of existence. At the end, as he waves to shouting faces from his Dallas motorcade, the Texas Book Depository looms ahead, and we want to shout and alter the car's speed, or do any little thing that would make this black moment emerge in some other manner. But the precariousness and uncertainty of life smash in upon us, and the mournful beat of drums resumes again.

This film captures fleeting images that make up the paradigmatic event: little John hands his mother a book he is carrying and then salutes; Cardinal Cushing brushes away a tear; Mrs. Kennedy walks with firmness down Pennsylvania Avenue; the President plays with his children, always seeming to favor his back, which we now know caused him considerable pain; the riderless horse prances behind the casket, struggling to get away from his youthful military attendant, who resolutely keeps his face forward, somehow conscious of his own minor role in history.

That, finally, is what this film is: a reminder that we have all experienced one of those events that alter the course of history with such dramatic force that only some "mysterious other" could possibly make sense of its place in the total scheme. We had expected more of Kennedy than we had a right to expect, and this film reminds us again that in our grief we are destined to live always between the unattainable and the unknown, caught somewhere between heaven and earth, never at home on earth because even John Kennedy could not control life and never certain of heaven because this unthinkable thing was allowed to happen to us.

A film made with a limited budget for overseas propaganda must, I suppose, bear the marks of oversimplification, faulty writing, and weak transitions. It would be difficult to make a bad film out of this subject, but it is to the credit of producer George Stevens, Jr., that he went beyond the routine and made a very good picture. Aimed at overseas audiences, the film needs Peck's careful narration regarding the Alliance for Progress or Kennedy's zeal for peace. In this sense, the picture has special merit for future American school children who will want to try to put the Kennedy years in perspective. But this simplicity is also the film's great drawback. Even for propaganda purposes it is offensive to have the Bay of Pigs brushed aside in one sentence. And the presentation of the civil rights movement is chronologically confusing, ending with the March on Washington with large crowds listening intently while Kennedy's voice comes over the soundtrack, even though, as the narrator notes, Kennedy met personally only with the march leaders and did not address the crowds. The fondness of developing nations for Abraham Lincoln is exploited, with interspersed shots of Lincoln's statue viewing the funeral procession. It might have been appropriate for Bill Mauldin's cartoon to have that statue weeping the day after the murder, but three years later this linking of Kennedy to Lincoln is too theatrical to contribute toward interpretative history.

Peck's narration, moving from the administration's six major achievements back to the funeral procession, suffers at times from amateurish touches. The script moves from excited Costa Rican crowds to the funeral by telling us that Kennedy will "never again stand on Latin American soil." This is a maudlin and shallow use of the film's post-event advantages; besides, it is meaningless, since events other than his death might have prevented Kennedy's return to Latin America.

But these are minor flaws, hardly enough to overshadow such effective documentary touches as the funeral cortege filmed from varying vantage points or the wild movement of a hand-held camera at the moment the assassin strikes. As a simple, emotion-laden, yet discreet examination of the brief presidency and tragic death of John F. Kennedy, this is a valuable document.   *(June 30, 1966)*

Persona (Svensk Filmindustri Production)
Directed by Ingmar Bergman; starring Bibi Andersson and Liv Ullmann.

In much of his recent work, Ingmar Bergman seems to be focusing on the problem of modern man living without God. In his trilogy — *Through a Glass Darkly, Winter Light,* and *The Silence* — he moves from a statement that God is to be equated with love to an outright admission that God is silent.

Now, in *Persona,* Bergman suggests that his characters have lost God because they have experienced a severe separation within themselves. This separation is none other than that traditional conflict of his early Lutheran parsonage training — the battle between spirit and flesh. It is not the departure of God as a concept that bothers Bergman, but the absence of any being or power capable of restoring man to wholeness, a redemption, if you will, that could successfully blend the flesh and the spirit without losing the values of either.

In *The Silence* Bergman seemed to be telling the story

of two sisters, an intellectual and a sensualist, who were bound together in a lesbian relationship finally broken by the departure of the sensual sister while her older sister lies dying in an isolated hotel room. Some critics have noted that, rather than a conflict between two sisters, Bergman meant to suggest an internal conflict between flesh and spirit, housed in a single personality. His two characters were so clearly delineated, however, that most of his public preferred to accept the two girls as separate entities.

The two girls in *Persona,* however, merge at times into one single personality, suggesting that Bergman has either settled for a psychological case study of confused personalities or has attempted to paint a portrait of a single personality, driven to a mental hospital over her failure to resolve the spirit-flesh conflict. Some critics have suggested that the girls "swap" personalities, but the more likely explanation — especially in the light of his treatment of Anna and Ester in *The Silence* — is that Bergman's girls represent a struggle for supremacy within a single soul.

Persona ostensibly is "about" a young actress, Elisabeth Vogler (Liv Ullmann), who suddenly loses her ability to speak. Acknowledging that this is but a retreat from reality, her doctor assigns a young nurse, Alma (Bibi Andersson), to the case and sends the two of them away to a summer home on the coast. Alma, at first solicitous and kind, begins to talk about her own life to Elisabeth, sharing with her a vivid description of a four-way sexual orgy on the beach. Elisabeth, who is silent throughout, finally provokes Alma to deep hostility, especially after Alma intercepts and reads a letter she has written that suggests that their relationship has lesbian overtones.

If *Persona* is a statement of internal conflict between spirit and flesh, Bergman has done a masterful job of examining one complex personality conducting an internal dialogue with herself. The nurse (sensual) tries to be aware of herself by talking to the actress (spiritual) and facing some of the elements of her life that have led to her mental illness. Bergman conveys this with breathtaking cinematic skill.

In an opening sequence, a young boy tosses in his bed until he awakens and gropes toward a large blow-up of a woman behind his head. When the boy's groping fades into the inside of a movie projector, we are left with the impression that Bergman is about to use his particular medium to tell us something of his own child-based internal struggle. Again, at a crucial point in the Elisabeth-Alma conflict, the film appears to snap and we enter briefly into a replay of early, frantic silent films. It is at this point that Alma discovers her patient is "using" her (a similar moment occurs to Karin in *Through a Glass*

Persona

Darkly), and this sense of being used without being accepted causes Alma's world to snap. Since she lives within the film image, what snaps is the celluloid in the projector.

Here Bergman suggests that the one thing the human spirit cannot tolerate is to find itself used, either by others, or through some insidious self-deception. In the conflict between the two women in this film, the misuse is a retreat into spiritual existence without assuming any responsibility for the sensual which brings both pleasure and pain. Bergman brings his heroine out of her schizophrenia onto the side of the sensual by having Alma walk away from the cottage after telling Elisabeth that beyond life there is "nothing." Here perhaps is Bergman's metaphysical statement: nothing judges or condemns. There is only life to be lived, and man must come to accept himself as he is in order to receive the gift of wholeness.

In this connection it should be remembered that Karin, hovering on the brink of mental illness in *Through a Glass Darkly,* tells her father that she cannot live in two worlds at the same time. She elects the world of unreality and therefore gives up life, in part because when God finally did come to her it was in the form of a huge spider. For Karin, the shock of a God who disappoints leads to total schizophrenia.

But in *Persona* Alma elects life, just as Anna in *The Silence* chose to continue on without her sick sister. In both films the acceptance of the sensual is possible only when it is informed, but not dominated, by the spiritual insight that love is essential. Bergman has thus performed the delicate task of resolving the spirit-flesh conflict in favor of flesh accepted for what it is, but sustained by the need for love.

Much has been said of Bergman's great skill at depicting women. If my thesis is correct — if both *The Silence* and *Persona* are artistic statements about himself — then Bergman is not describing the psychological makeup of women in either film. He is rather using the feminine psyche to move more closely into his own existence, on the assumption that the artist is more accurately understood as a female, possessing the qualities of tenderness, openness, sensitivity, and vulnerability that our society normally attributes to the female. Besides, a girl-girl relationship does not carry the emotional "threat" of a boy-boy experience, at least not in our society.

Bergman is not interested in the feminine or masculine "role," any more than he cares about his girls in *Persona* as "nurse" and "actress." As in his previous trilogy, he isolates his major characters, separating them from conventional ties to society and lays bare their (his) internal struggle. In the Swedish tradition of August Strindberg, Bergman continues to brood over his unresolved Lutheran pietistic conflict between pure spirit and carnal desire. Most adults manage to achieve some resolution of this conflict, but Bergman's curse is that he is an artist, and each time he sets image to screen he finds the same struggle facing him.

(June 15, 1967)

The Graduate (Embassy)
Produced by Lawrence Turman; directed by Mike Nichols; starring Dustin Hoffman, Anne Bancroft, Katherine Ross.

At first glance this is a pretty wild piece of cinema. Its surface plot is bizarre, like somebody's commercial idea of a new trend in sensationalism. But *The Graduate* is much more than a plot film. It is a work of cinematic art that presents a vision of contemporary life through a mixture of sharp comedy sketches, devastating attacks on suburban apathy, and effective use of Simon and Garfunkel's folk-rock compositions.

Mike Nichols is the director, his second effort (after *Who's Afraid of Virginia Woolf?*), and once again his skills are used to slice away the overwhelming *acedia* — not caring — that creeps over our landscape like a plague. The graduate of the title is Benjamin, a 20-year-old honor student (Dustin Hoffman), who arrives home from college with a vacant stare and a sense of unrelatedness to the superficial, affluent world of his parents. The tone is set as the Simon and Garfunkel tune "Sounds of Silence" underscores Benjamin's flight home to Los Angeles, an evocative comment that announces the film's theme: people live with one another without being present to anyone.

The plot of this presentational film is from a novel, and it serves as a substructure for Nichols' camera artistry. Best that the plot go unreported, but since the mass media will delight in its every irrelevant detail, a brief sketching is in order. Benjamin is seduced by an older woman (Anne Bancroft), the wife of his father's business partner, and this affair serves to focus for him the vacuity of his life against the possibilities of what might be. The nature of this genuine life is never clear to him, though it is symbolized by a young girl who becomes the object of a frantic search.

Dustin Hoffman is excellent as the young graduate who is turned off by the prospects of a life encompassed by demands that have no meaning and loyalties that are unimportant. Nichols' direction highlights facial reactions, a technique that minimizes surroundings and emphasizes faces that love and hate without emotion. In an early scene, the young graduate stares into a fish aquarium, contemplating the restrictive fin-life and resisting his parents' entreaties to enter the cocktail party fishbowl downstairs. When he does go down, he is bombarded by well-wishing that is studied and joyless, apathetic in its role of non-caring. One successful business-type pulls Benjamin aside, and with earnestness one would expect to hover around a subject of life or death, he tells the youth that he has only one word for him: *plastics*.

Declining this and all industrial panaceas, Benjamin seeks his own answer to the *acedia* that he possesses as part of his heritage. He thinks he finds it in a beautiful young girl, played by Katherine Ross, who is perfect as the un-committed female programmed into a future exactly like her parents' loveless existence.

The laughter of this film is misleading, for the after-effect is extremely depressing. Nichols has provided an unrelenting comment on what happens to us when we sub-stitute routine for love and demand conformity rather than humanity. The photography is excellent, the editing appropriately fast, and the performances outstanding. The musical score by Paul Simon and Art Garfunkel is exactly right, and will hopefully give these young poetic prophets the kind of mass recognition they deserve.

(January 11, 1968)

The Green Berets (Warner Brothers-Seven Arts)
Produced by Michael Wayne; directed by John Wayne and Ray Kellogg; starring John Wayne, David Janssen, Jim Hutton.

A critic who opposes the present United States strategy in Vietnam is naturally suspect in reviewing a film that is heavily and woodenly pro-war. And this is precisely why *The Green Berets* is such a bad film. It is so overly sim-plistic that the alternative to its point of view is treason.

Surely the presence of 500,000 American servicemen at war in a distant land is an event deserving sensitive cine-matic treatment. The war is politically ambiguous, but the dying and killing remain a personal story of anguish, suf-fering, and guilt. It deserves examination, indeed, but un-fortunately John Wayne, serving as star and director of this film, has chosen to look at Vietnam, 1968, through the narrow, prejudiced vision of World War II, 1944.

Remember those simple days when "Japs" were vicious and cruel soldiers who raped little children? Well, John Wayne has decided that this view of the enemy applies to the Viet Cong. Remember the American West, divided into two camps — the fighting Indians who massacred and muti-lated and the gentle Indians who only wanted protection inside the fort? They are here again, and this time there is particular irony in Wayne's use of this image of the benev-olent white man protecting the good Indian from his bad cousins.

Wayne based his film on Robin Moore's novel, *The Green Berets*. He avoids the problem of competing with the contemporary headlines by placing his story back in the days when American troops were called advisors to "help" the South Vietnamese. The film was shot in Fort Benning, Georgia, with the obvious help and support of U.S. military men and equipment, a pattern the govern-ment has long followed for filmmakers who are making propaganda films.

And this finally is what the film is, a piece of propa-ganda in favor of the war. But it need not have been this bad. Wayne has starred in some good films as an actor, the slow-talking hero who oozes confidence and guarantees an exciting and ultimately successful ending. But as a director Wayne has allowed his patriotism to box him into an im-possible corner. Vietnam is not World War II, as we saw it back then. It is not over, and we are not winning. So when he "moves out," it is an empty gesture that no amount of killing will overcome.

In clumsy fashion Wayne has actually made two films. The first is an episode against the Viet Cong. They drive us out, but the cavalry — which is to say, an airplane with heavy machine guns — wipes them out and shoots down their flag, which is red (instead of the Rising Sun). Along the way, the country boy — the lieutenant who was to go home the next day — and the brave, Commie-hating Vietnamese commander are killed. They are clichés, legitimate if used to project a vision or support a story. Here they are only badly connected moments from old war movies.

In the second episode, Wayne's men capture a Viet Cong officer with the careful planning of *The Dirty Dozen,* and then send him away with a nice James Bond touch, airborne in a parachute. This episode is less concerned with underlining our right to be in Vietnam and is directed with more care. I suspect that Wayne's assistant director handled these segments.

There is nothing wrong with plot films, even when divided into two episodes. But the plot should have some finesse, providing surprises and maintaining interest. In *The Green Berets,* it is clear from the very outset that the dovish correspondent (David Janssen) is going to be the foil Wayne has to convert over to the hawk side. What is left for the plot is the "how" of the conversion. But even this is telegraphed when Janssen gives a little Vietnamese girl a medal he is wearing. Sure enough, a few scenes later she is the girl raped by five Viet Cong soldiers.

The style of filmmaking Wayne represents is further illustrated when he breaks the news to Janssen about the rape. He spares our sensitive ears from hearing the real word and tells Janssen the girl has been "assaulted." This concern to protect his audience verbally is preceded by scenes of soldiers dying in various and colorful ways. Parents will be delighted to know that not only will the children not hear the word "rape," but that scarcely a word of profanity is uttered by these specimens of U. S. fighting men. They garrote, burn, machine-gun, and torture, but they don't cuss. And your six-year-old won't know what has happened to the girl. It has all been implied in grown-up talk. He can't miss the burning soldiers, however.

Another happy holdover from World War II is the soldier who scrounges and is a hero for his actions. What he really does is steal, of course, but you recall that in big wars this is okay. The scrounger, by the way, befriends a little Vietnamese boy who has a dog. The dog is killed, milking a few cheap tears from the audience. The boy lives, but the scrounger dies, which of course sets up Wayne to tell the little boy that he will not be left alone, for after all, he is "what this is all about."

A cynical friend who had not seen this film commented to me, "Well, I suppose it ends with old John going off into the sunset to the strains of the 'Song of the Green Berets.' " Gentle reader, I must admit, that is exactly the way it ends.

(July 11, 1968)

Midnight Cowboy (United Artists)
Produced by Jerome Hellman; directed by John Schlesinger; starring Dustin Hoffman and Jon Voight. MPAA rating: X

Last Summer (Allied Artists)
Directed by Frank Perry; written by Eleanor Perry; starring Cathy Burns. MPAA rating: X.

Dwight MacDonald distinguishes a critic and a reviewer by identifying a critic as a writer who says how he likes a film, while a reviewer concerns himself with his reader's potential reaction. I am not sure that I buy this separation, but in today's market no one writing about films can avoid reminding his readers that for some of them a given picture is must-see, while for others it is must-avoid. These two films are important, but they are not for casual entertainment.

Midnight Cowboy, by far the better of the two, is easily one of the best films of this year — for some viewers. Joe Buck (Jon Voight) is a Texas cowboy who comes to New York City because he considers himself a great lover. He assumes that rich ladies are waiting to pay him for his favors. In the process of discovering that they are not, he meets Ratso (Dustin Hoffman), a wily dreg from 42nd Street. When Joe's money runs out, Ratso invites him to share a room in an abandoned building, and these two disparate personalities establish the kind of emotional

Midnight Cowboy

bond that reveals that man in any condition is capable of love, loyalty, and compassion.

The acting of Hoffman (in a totally different role from his in *The Graduate)* and Voight is superb as they develop a firm bond, meaningful in the simple process of sharing soup, dirty mattresses, and dreams of the future. Director John Schlesinger's eye for New York detail provides heart-rending authenticity, uncovering aspects of Fun City you don't read about in *The New Yorker.* Unfortunately, the film has lapses that slow it down, marring its total impact. As the relationship between the two men builds past the middle of the film, this mood is garishly interrupted by a psychedelic interlude staged by some of Andy Warhol's performers. Dramatically, this sequence serves to speed the pair's decision to go to Florida, but it is unnecessary, and its presence in the latter half of the film causes a break in the pacing and a disturbing pause in the momentum. Schlesinger is either unable to edit out his indulgence in special effects, or his backer urged the interlude to make the film more "entertaining." Whatever, it is only a minor intrusion, and does not greatly detract from a moving cinematic document of the corruption of an eager youth and the resulting renewal he gains from his relationship to the apparently unlovable Ratso.

Midnight Cowboy is an important film, and anyone concerned with film as an art form should not miss it. It is not recommended, however, for the casual filmgoer who would be unprepared for the realism and treatment of the life of a temporary male hustler in the backwash of New York's neon-lit streets.

Last Summer is also about innocence defiled, but whereas *Midnight Cowboy* projects a vision of hope, *Last Summer* ends as an exercise in despair. Four young teenagers are idling away the summer, spending, as the title suggests, their last summer of innocence. Frank Perry *(David and Lisa)* once again reveals a sensitive touch with young performers — in this case, two handsome, tanned blond boys, a future socialite brunette, and Rhoda, the ugly duckling of the quartet, a winsome, plump blonde played with restrained brooding by Cathy Burns.

Miss Burns, in fact, is the film's most redeeming feature, as she struggles to retain her own sense of identity against the pressures of the trio's mindless and vicious notion of summer fun. Eleanor Perry's script has moments of honesty when she captures the teen-age milieu. The youngsters themselves, with their mixture of innocence and cynical wisdom, make this an engrossing film.

The three attractive teen-agers form a bond of truth, and when this becomes boring they turn on Miss Burns as a scapegoat, angry that she is different, and frustrated that she is reluctant to follow their senseless immorality. In the film's ugly and disturbing conclusion, they assault her in a scene reminiscent of the rape in *The Virgin Spring.* I understand this scene is to be cut some in order to gain the film an R, rather than an X rating. Cuts are needed, because Perry's notion of this kind of violence is a screenful of bare bodies and large facial close-ups. I hope this cutting will produce the kind of restraint Bergman used in *The Virgin Spring,* suggesting the horror of rape without dwelling at length on its details.

I also wish Perry had avoided the heavy double symbolism of an injured seagull and the violated young girl — two "innocents" helped and then crushed by the trio. In addition, I can't really feel that the rape scene was needed to show Rhoda's destruction. Not that the rape could not have happened, but simply that it is too gross and too large a jump dramatically from earlier teen cruelties to this, the ultimate cruel act.

The serious filmgoer will want to see *Last Summer,* if only to ponder the question of what has happened to Perry since *David and Lisa.* Have his commercial failures in Hollywood moved him from the hope of his David saving

Lisa from mental alienation to the rape and despair of *Last Summer?*

(*July 24, 1969*)

Easy Rider (Columbia Pictures)
Produced by Peter Fonda; directed by Dennis Hopper; starring Peter Fonda and Dennis Hopper. MPAA rating: R.

The personal film is moving out of the underground into commercial theaters. Slowly — ever so slowly — major companies are putting a little money into the hands of young, creative people and giving them control over personal film projects. *Easy Rider* is the latest and perhaps the most significant personal film to date. It is produced by Peter Fonda with some modest encouragement from Columbia Pictures, which is distributing the film and basking in the long lines and box office returns that are mounting.

Easy Rider cost $375,000, which — as films go — is dirt

Last Summer

cheap. A potboiler that runs as the second film on a double bill will probably cost around $1 million, and the really big ones, like *Dr. Doolittle,* can run as high as $20 million. When you consider that your ticket for *Easy Rider* costs as much as the ticket for *Dr. Doolittle,* you begin to get some idea of the difference in profits; and since profit is the name of the game, the personal film is beginning to make itself felt in those offices in New York where money decisions are made.

A personal film eschews formula. It reflects the point of view of the filmmaker, telling "his thing" as he wants to tell it. If what he has to say is pointless, then the public will ignore him. But Fonda and his director and costar Dennis Hopper are saying something through their film that is touching at least a portion of the public's psyche. They are doing so with a cinematic skill that reflects years of experience around movie lots, despite their youth. And they have touched a responsive chord in the filmgoing generation, the 16 to 30 crowd.

Easy Rider is an odyssey of two long-haired bearded types — Fonda and Hopper — who strike it rich in the West. That their loot comes from a large sale of cocaine is itself a commentary on the American Dream; success and money are more important than the values in the sale. Riding their motorcycle steeds eastward, they retrace the American frontier, moving from Los Angeles back to New Orleans. (The film is not without its faults: a shot of a horse being shod in the foreground with the boys fixing a motorcycle flat tire in the background is a little too obvious.)

The personal film has little plot, only the gradual revelation of human interaction. *Easy Rider* seems to meander, moving with the cyclists through a hippie commune in New Mexico, through Texas, and into Louisiana, by which time a third man has joined the journey, an alcoholic lawyer (Jack Nicholson). As the verbal philosopher in the film Nicholson sums up what the film is all about — a bad trip through a land whose dream has died. Actually, Nicholson's commentary is a concession to the movieland tradition, since cinematically the film had already cast the spell of ennui that its makers wanted to project.

Fonda calls himself Wyatt, and his companion is Billy, suggesting again disillusionment with the past and rejection of Western heroes whose exploits ushered in a modernity that has no values but the dollar and the bitch goddess success. What makes Fonda's film so important, however, is not just his comment that the dream is lost, but the fact that his film has an integrity and an authenticity to his particular point of view. Except for the excesses in the LSD trip sequence near the end, the picture makes few concessions to formula audiences. There is no blatant nudity, no romantic involvement, no excessive violence, just a revelation of one man's vision, realized on a modest and somewhat limited artistic scale. If the film succeeds commercially, other film companies may start looking around for talented producers and directors with something to say, the ability to say it cinematically, and the audience receptive to the vision they present.

(October 16, 1969)

Paint Your Wagon (Paramount)
Produced by Alan Jay Lerner; directed by Joshua Logan; starring Lee Marvin, Clint Eastwood, and Jean Seberg. MPAA rating: GP.

If you are worried about dirty movies, I have just the one for you. *Paint Your Wagon* is a $20 million exercise in group vulgarity, tastelessness, and flagrant hostility to God and religion. If a "dirty" movie can be defined as a film that disdains sex, God, and mankind in general, then this must be the most expensive dirty movie ever made.

What makes this an added insult to sex, God, and man is the context. The seedy little sexploitation films that grind out their weary existence on the edges of our major cities are pathetic, hardly noticed except by the lonely men who slip in and out hoping for brief glimpses of erotica. But *Paint Your Wagon* is bigness, spread out in all its vulgarity as a roadshow attraction, complete with fancy overture, big stars, reserved seats, expensive tickets, and the kind of intermission that helps create a Broadway mood: smartly dressed ladies and expense-account men repeating the hilariously funny things they have just seen.

Subject matter *per se* is never what turns me against a film. *Midnight Cowboy* dealt with a sordid theme, but its treatment was sensitive and finally redemptive. *Easy Rider* centered on a cross-country odyssey financed by drugs, but the film's vision was essentially positive. *Paint Your Wagon* contains none of those scenes that usually upset people (like bare skin), but I left the theater with the feeling that I had been personally degraded and insulted. It is not the subject matter that makes it a bad film, it is the unbelievably dirty treatment of that subject matter. The plot — Lee Marvin buying a wife (Jean Seberg) from a Mormon and sharing her with his gold-mining partner in an 1870 California gold-mining camp might have been handled with finesse. The humor might have focused on the institution of marriage, for certainly anything that commands so much of our emotions is a prime target for foible-tapping. But *Paint Your Wagon* merely uses this three-way marriage to leer. It does not seek to enlighten, entertain, or amuse. Rather, it revolves for three full hours around the horniness (that's the film's word, not mine) of a gold-mining camp without women. Since Marvin and Eastwood are sharing the only woman in camp, a raid is made on a stagecoach bearing six French prostitutes, and the ladies are brought back to the camp to set up their business. Again, the brothel is standard Western fare, but in the Western genre the brothel is background like trees and sky, not a major subplot.

The cynical attacks on God and religion deserve special attention. Bumbling ministers and pietistic laymen are longstanding easy comedy targets. They deserve to be because they are misusing the Christian faith. But this picture's humor is a direct attack on God, laughing not at misinterpretations of Him, but at Him. *Bedazzled* was a successful satire on religion because it exhibited a basic respect for that which lay behind the material under attack — misplaced ideas of God and confused church patterns. But Marvin's running battle against God establishes his own immoral life as superior to any religious practice, confused or straight. Sneering at God for mistreating the living, Marvin delivers a funeral oration. Noting some gold dust beside the freshly dug grave, the pallbearers throw the body aside with the kind of flippancy once seen in silent film comedies. An itinerant preacher arrives to condemn the sinners, and his homiletical language is not funny because it is directly from scriptural material that does not deserve attack. Humor cannot be directed at the undeserving and still be both funny and respectful. The man who falls on the banana peel cannot be weak; he must be pompous.

There are other lapses that defeat any possibility of humor in the material at hand. The French prostitutes are conducting a thriving business. But one girl is shown in the kind of embrace now associated with orgy scenes, jarring the viewer out of the bawdy mood into a brief suggestion of eroticism. Marvin introduces the son of a pious farmer to the joys of whisky, smoking, and women, in that order. The boy says he likes the last best. So far, unpleasant, but if stopped here, at least bearable. But the film continues with Marvin informing the boy's parents of their son's adventure, and of course the parents look foolish in their protests while Marvin's views on life are made to be superior. The objections raised to this exchange by Marvin's wife and by Eastwood are weak in comparison to Marvin's zestful defense of sin. This, then, is the film's immorality. It verbally pretends that Marvin is wrong, but visually portrays him as clearly the superior being. Standard sex comedy stuff: give the audience the vulgarity and titillation they want, but leave them with surface morality to assuage what little conscience may still be operative.

Cinematically the film is a disaster. It cost $20 million to produce, and instead of moving out more into the spacious landscape of California (the film's actual shooting was in Oregon), most of the money was spent on studio stuff — saloons, mining camp streets, and an underground tunnel. This tunnel, by the way, is dug to capture gold dust falling through the floors of the various bars. It sets up the film's finale when a wild steer charges through the tunnel, knocking down supports and causing the entire sinful city to fall into the ground below.

Logan's direction is static. He doesn't pan across the long wagon train shots: he merely cuts in closer and closer, crying out with the obviousness of set shots. One exception: a drunk Marvin awakes to see the first woman in camp. He raises to a nearby stream, stands stiff on the bank, and falls headlong into the water, floats a few feet, and gets up. The stream shot is continuous, no cutting, and the humor is effective and sustained. Marvin has some moments of dry wit and poignancy, telling Eastwood to stay by him when he is drunk in the mud and when he gets melancholy. But these are isolated moments, inundated in a wasteful, distasteful extravagance that I hope loses most of that $20 million investment.

As I said, there is no nudity — absolutely none. The language is vulgar and gratuitous. All the nonleads are Broadway cardboard characters, and there is absolutely no sense of the gold mine era in the film. What a terrible waste of money.

(December 11, 1969)

Patton (Twentieth-Century Fox)
Produced by Frank McCarthy; directed by Franklin J. Schaffner; starring George C. Scott and Karl Malden. MPAA rating: GP.

The first image in *Patton* is a giant United States flag, the backdrop to a stage. Slowly, from the rear, General George Patton emerges, covered with ribbons and dressed in that handsome uniform that anyone over forty will remember with nostalgia. In a brief speech to the audience (spoken as though we were about to go into battle), General Patton (superbly played by George C. Scott) tells us that war is glorious, and that Americans never lose because they love war. The effect is stunning — a masterful directorial stroke. To a nation disgusted with the Vietnam War, but still remembering World War II and its glory, *Patton* at the outset informs us that the glory of war is in the eye of the beholder.

This is not a picture that argues for or against combat. It is rather a portrayal of a man with a single-minded obsession, pursued with the fanaticism and intensity that produces success, but that also carries with it the instability that leads finally to destruction. Men like Patton have always been crucial for winning wars because in their fanaticism they do not pause to wonder why, they simply push ahead to victory. In the midst of war we revere them; in peacetime we reject them, because without the heat of anger they are an anachronism.

Producer Frank McCarthy, himself a retired brigadier

119

general and a former aide to General Marshall, correctly assessed the Patton phenomenon as devotion to a single cause rather than as an obsession with war or a delight with death. He presents Patton in a sympathetic light without condoning war, a remarkable feat possible only because he chose to paint a "portrait of a rebel" — rather than of a war hero.

This picture is filled with subtle touches that make it a joyous experience to anyone captivated by the wonder that is man. Director Franklin Schaffner (who showed his skill in *The Planet of the Apes*) gives us little moments that make a rewarding whole only after we have passed through the experience. Consider a sequence prior to and highlighting Patton's first combat in the North African campaign. He has been given command of the American tank forces after their disastrous defeat at Kasserine Pass. Two aides slip quietly into his bedroom; one opens the blinds, the other shakes him gently awake. The old soldier opens his eyes widely. He is told that Rommel is coming to attack. Patton throws back the covers, revealing that he is sleeping with his clothes on, waiting for this moment. Beside his bed is a book written by Rommel describing his tank tactics. In the battle that follows, the Germans are surrounded and badly defeated. From the hillside, Patton watches with grim glee, and when victory is assured, he can barely contain his excitement, exclaiming, "Rommel, you —, I read your *book*!"

This is, of course, how single-minded men succeed. They do not mow the lawn or tuck the children in bed at night. They have no time for small talk. They are, in fact, terrible human beings, except when they are accomplishing what we want them to accomplish — winning football games or wars, arranging corporation mergers, writing plays.

I don't know how younger viewers will receive *Patton,* but I hope they will sense something of the gloriousness that their parents felt about World War II. Then maybe they will be less harsh on us for taking that same mentality and trying to apply it to Vietnam, where it simply will not work. This view of war as sacred and exciting had no business working in 1941-45 either, but it did, and as a result Hitler was defeated.

Patton's flaws are appropriate to the style of the film, which keeps Patton center-stage. British Field Marshal Bernard Montgomery is a foppish little fellow who stumbled into victory so that the British would have a hero. Patton, on the other hand, is the supreme warrior, stupid in politics, but superb in battle. His admission that he is uninterested in politics appears distorted, otherwise why would the real Patton have made so many remarks against the Russians or had such precise notions as to how the war should be won?

Indeed, the film's real villains are newspaper reporters whose reports turn Patton's foibles into negative headlines. Its view of the misunderstood leader in the hands of a rapacious press rings flat. The picture is finally pro-Patton in that it gives him much more self-awareness than he probably deserves. His admission that he loves war, "God help me," evokes audience sympathy rather than distrust, and his admission that he "knows" that his outbursts inspire his men softens the suggestion that his behavior is uncontrolled.

Director Schaffner depicts war with objective appropriateness, seeing it with an awareness that the carnage is there, but that those who die are part of the greater victorious whole. This is Patton's view, and Schaffner does not break rhythm by suggesting otherwise. The only soldier we actually know before he dies is a Patton aide, struck down by an 88-mm. shell after delivering a message from his leader. He goes to his death with the zeal of a halfback rushing in to tell the quarterback that now is the time to throw the bomb. And a grieving Patton clearly mourns the

loss of a faithful servant and an able soldier rather than the death of a man.

The film's closing scene is a remarkable unfolding of a man whose time has passed. Walking through the emptiness of a peacetime parade ground, Patton meets with his wartime comrade, General Omar Bradley (whose gentleness has provided a soft contrast to the harsh victory-mindedness of Patton). They visit together, and then Patton goes off for a lonely walk with his faithful dog, moving toward a windmill in the plains. If the symbolism of that windmill does not hit the viewer until several days later, then the picture's quixotic benediction to the end of an era of glorious battles will have had its proper effect.

Patton may well be the ultimate war film, the portrait of a man who does our dirty business because he loves it. We hate what he does, but we don't face this reality until he has finished his job.

(April 2, 1970)

Mississippi Mermaid (United Artists)
Directed by Francois Truffaut; starring Catherine Deneuve and Jean-Paul Belmondo. MPAA rating: GP.

Back in the earlier days when non-American film directors brought their films to these shores, they usually obtained distribution through some small company and considered themselves fortunate if the film got into a majority of the "art" theaters in large cities and around college towns. Those were the days when Bergman, Fellini, and Antonioni were known only to the *cognoscenti.* Alas, commerce inevitably reared its wicked head, and the subtitled film began to be either atrociously dubbed or the director encouraged to make his picture in English.

Francois Truffaut, a 38-year-old French director, ventured into this uncertain terrain only once, translating Ray Bradbury's science fiction novel *Fahrenheit 451* into an English-language film. The result was an artistic and commercial disappointment. Truffaut has fortunately returned to France and now makes only French-language films, the latest of which is *Mississippi Mermaid*. The small distribution companies of an earlier day have gone the way of most small companies; thus Truffaut must make his way into the American market through the distribution facilities of United Artists. Unfortunately United Artists has given no evidence that it knows the value of this particular product, and if its limited New York showing is any example, the rest of the country will probably have to watch very carefully lest it miss seeing *Mississippi Mermaid* altogether.

This film does require a particular orientation because it is simply not to be taken on a literal level. You can say this much about an obvious commercial film like *The Adventurers* or *Airport:* They have absolutely no subtlety. They hit the audience with all the finesse of a Mack truck. Truffaut, on the other hand, is a film artist. He uses the medium to share an artistic vision with his audience. He is an interesting filmmaker in that the two major influences on him were Alfred Hitchcock and Jean Renoir. This strange cinematic ancestry has lured him into a form in which the plot bears certain Hitchcockian touches, encompassed in the warm impressionistic colors of a Renoir film. He also has the unfortunate habit of relying for plot on the most superficial of novels, thus giving the impression that he may very well be making a conventional potboiler film.

Mississippi Mermaid, for example, is drawn from a Cornell Woolrich novel that tells of a French plantation owner's marriage to a girl he met through the want ads. It is obvious from the outset that this marriage is based on a deception, and the husband takes slightly longer than the audience to discover this. The girl who arrives on the island of Reunion, where Jean-Paul Belmondo (the husband) runs a tobacco plantation, is not the bride he ordered. Little clues are dropped to tell us this, and an impression is left that Truffaut is going to give us a Hitchcock-style film where horror lurks in the simple details of a dying canary or a wife who prefers coffee to tea. But Truffaut is finally not Hitchcock, and he is using this tale of a marriage deception to paint a cinematic portrait of a woman whose beauty and fragility are so enslaving that neither the deceived husband nor the audience dares to reject her, no matter what she does to us.

My favorite Truffaut film is *Jules and Jim,* and I think I am particularly drawn to *Mississippi Mermaid* because there is a resemblance between Catherine Deneuve's power of enslavement and that of Jeanne Moreau in *Jules and Jim.* In both instances Truffaut is communicating an insight into human character, suggesting that the strength of love is such that it has the possibility of overcoming the most intolerable behavior patterns in those who are loved.

Watching Truffaut is an exciting experience because the viewer discovers that each incident possesses several levels of meaning. At the wedding, for example, the bride's wedding band is too small, since it was designed to fit the hand of the original correspondent, now sadly drowned at sea. In moistening her finger to force the ring on, Catherine Deneuve conveys to the audience both the surface fact that something is not in order, and a more sensual reality regarding the deceiver.

Again, when Belmondo, through the clumsy device of seeing his wife at a dance hall on television, decides to confront her with her deception, Truffaut allows the audience to experience the ambience of the wife's former and present life with a stunning single camera set-up that follows her from a third floor apartment out the front door, around a square, and into a cheap dance hall. Truffaut then has Belmondo check the door of the dance hall, turn and go across the street, and climb on the out-side of the building into a window, where he awaits her return. The beauty of this scene lies in the evocation of dread and attraction, the communication of an environ-ment, and — for good measure — a remarkable acrobatic feat of scaling the outside of an apartment building. This entire sequence is necessary to the plot, but even more necessary to the establishment of the darkness of the hus-band's mood and the final fadeout before he confesses that he could not possibly murder his wife because, quite simply, he loves her. Her sad confession of why she has deceived him is soap opera material, except that Miss Deneuve communicates it with such sensitivity that only the most hardened viewer could reject her rationale.

I once conducted a film seminar and asked my students to describe *Jules and Jim* with one word after their viewing of the picture. Most of the class were male seminarians, and almost without exception their immediate reaction to *Jules and Jim* was "sad, chaotic, tragic, or morbid." A nun, visiting that evening, disagreed. She found it to be a film of joy. That a group of people could find both morbidity and joy in the same film is an indication of the value of Truffaut's art. He encompasses life in all of its dimensions and introduces the viewer to an experience of both joy and sadness in the same moment.

(May 28, 1970)

This Man Must Die (Allied Artists)
Directed by Claude Chabrol. MPAA rating: GP.

The film critic, like the educator, finds it difficult these days to convince an audience that he has something impor-tant to say. Gone are the days when docile classes or

126

readers (or even congregations) waited to hear some word on high from authorized experts. "The teacher says" used to be the final word on the playground. Now this is scoffed at as early as second grade.

Critics ought to be educators of a sort, suggesting different slants on films or uncovering new dimensions otherwise missed by the general audience. But in this anti-authority era, who listens? Which makes it all the more frustrating when a film like *This Man Must Die* comes along.

Here is a French-language picture (with English subtitles) that is, in my judgment, one of the four or five best films of this year, and almost no one will see it because it is not what it appears to be on the surface. The critic-

This Man Must Die

educator who stands in his seat and shouts for the world to listen probably will not impress even the second-graders. Here we are in this era of absolute freedom and rebellion against authority, and everyone uses his total license to talk about the same movies and adopt essentially the same mass reaction.

But again, like educators (and preachers), critics keep trying, hoping someone will pay attention, not to prove that they are correct, but because they want certain pictures to be experienced by the widest possible audience. (Richard Schickel, by the way, has already praised Chabrol's film in *Life,* so if you won't believe a religious critic, go and read him, for heaven's sake!)

Claude Chabrol directed. (If that does not mean anything to you, don't worry; it didn't mean anything to me either until I started studying films more than casually a few years ago.) Chabrol is one of the French New Wave directors, very much a master craftsman with a vision to be shared. His vision is not as revolutionary as Jean Luc Godard's, nor as grace-filled as Robert Bresson's, but it is a vision to receive and ponder because it commands attention at levels of feeling not often reached through popular media.

Chabrol is a film artist whose every frame is designed to ensnare the viewer and bring him into that mysterious realm the artist is prepared to share with all that risk the encounter. He does this within the conventional film structure of a thriller. The setting is a small village on the French coast. A young boy is killed by a hit-and-run driver. The grief-stricken father is enraged and sets out to find the killer and gain revenge.

But this is the form. The content is a vision shared. Seen briefly, the child embodies the joy of living, fishing by the vast sea, walking along the quiet village streets. A housekeeper, unable to remove the dead child's toys, breaks down and weeps, not hysterically, but with the conviction of one who has suffered a loss too deep to express. The French countryside, whose life pulsates, is set in sharp contrast to the cold, almost impersonal drive for revenge. A family scene, with a brutish father (the guilty driver) humiliating his wife and son, is painful in the extreme and absolutely correct.

Always there is the ocean, at first the locale of pleasure, then the place for plotting, and finally a symbol of the vastness of a world in which each man lives alone, even as he relies for meaning on others. The plot carries us forward to an ambiguous ending, not to tell a story or to entertain, but to engage and share.

Watch for *This Man Must Die*. It may show up at a nearby city (the *Life* review might guarantee that), or maybe in your local theater, if you encourage the manager to bring it in. It should be seen for its mastery of the film art, the tracking camera, the family portrait, the deliberate plot manipulation where coincidence guarantees plot movement.

It may also be felt for its portrayal of guilt transferred, or the theological question: Who is guilty — the killer or the hater? These are not characters who are described, but vehicles for the vision of the film artist. It is not a film that is "about" a search for revenge or even of a father's love for his son. It is rather a cinematic work knitted into a stylistic whole that has the potential of leading the viewer into a decision regarding his own life. Any film, or any man, who can do that deserves attention.

(October 15, 1970)

Carnal Knowledge (a Joseph E. Levine production, distributed by Avco-Embassy)
Produced and directed by Mike Nichols; starring Jack

Nicholson, Candice Bergen, Arthur Garfunkel, and Ann-Margret. MPAA rating: R.

You know the old saw from the non-filmgoer: "I don't need to see that film; I see enough of that in the people I have to deal with." *Carnal Knowledge* will probably produce this comment many times, for the film's central characters are very familiar types who behave in precisely the way you would expect them to behave.

Carnal Knowledge is a picture that appears on the surface to chuckle at man's sexual proclivities and then to express dismay over his excesses. I say "appears" because this fourth film from Mike Nichols neither chuckles nor expresses dismay. It *presents,* in Suzanne Langer's words, "the felt tensions of life, standing still to be looked at."

With this film, Mike Nichols has successfully evolved from his stage and cabaret background. He has infused the cinema form with his best from those earlier avenues of expression. Out of a tale of two college boys seeking the unobtainable love object, Nichols has produced a work of film art that employs the camera to let simple, shallow people reveal the deep anguish they feel over their inability to transcend their own pettiness. Displaying the childishness of man's serious purposes has long been a Nichols' trademark. His earlier cabaret interchanges with Elaine May ranged from the frustrated patient to the misunderstood NASA Mama's boy.

In the first film he directed, Nichols transferred the play *Who's Afraid of Virginia Woolf?* to the screen. In *The Graduate* and *Catch-22,* Nichols was finding his way in the film medium and at times was trapped between his own best instincts and the demands of commercial cinema. Now, with *Carnal Knowledge,* his evolving talent hits a major peak, for in this film he focuses with clinical precision on the simple but profound point that love is more than sexual conquest. But, you protest, I know that already. Yes, you may, but Nichols takes you on a journey through the life of two men who don't know it, and the anguish they cause themselves and others is finally a theological announcement that in other days might have been phrased as "the wages of sin is death."

Jack Nicholson and Arthur Garfunkel portray the two men. They are first seen as college seniors preening their way through the sexual jungle of one of those painful dances that colleges used to sponsor during the 1940s to allow boys and girls to meet one another. In subsequent scenes, the two men grow older; and we see them ten and twenty years after college, still moving through the jungle, but with rapidly decreasing success. Each turn in the downward spiral is so fraught with defeat and obvious disaster that one is immediately reminded of Dante's descent into hell. The closing scene — at once bizarre and pathetic — depicts the college stud as impotent: the ultimate degradation for a man who chooses the wrong object for his worship.

The reason that this is not just another journey through the lives of people you already know is Nichols' ability to draw from his performers portrayals that disclose depths of cruelty and fear not visible even to an interested observer. Candice Bergen, as the first girl the two men encounter, is seen in one long close-up, laughing uncontrollably at inane remarks that she exchanges with the two boys in a restaurant. Rather than cutting to the others, Nichols keeps the camera on Miss Bergen, watching her face as her laughter boils over and then slows down, turning to momentary uncertainty and then fear before she begins to laugh again. This exposure of a girl trying to hold two men, playing with ideals she doesn't feel, could have been missed if the camera had watched her companions for even a moment. But Nichols is unrelenting: he wants the viewer to know at the outset the penalty of absolute selfishness.

Nichols shows his mastery of film technique in the way he begins at a polite distance from his performers, establishing the childlikeness of the men in a shot of them discussing Miss Bergen in silhouette, outlined in front of a dormitory door. As the men grow older, the camera moves in closer, frequently remaining in single closeups that permit the performers to stare into the camera, confessing their waning grasp on reality. The film's strong sense of the cruelty of self-centeredness is accentuated by the virtual exclusion from screen of all but the intense faces of the performers. The shift in camera perspective from the photography of environment to facial close-ups heightens the sense of a Dantean spiral into hell, moving toward the closing shot of Nicholson's face, trapped in a final degrading moment with a prostitute.

Because this is a picture concerned to trace the futility of loveless sex, the script by Jules Feiffer contains some of the most specific, clinical references to sex that have been presented in this age of frankness. But the material is honest, and the visual scenes are restrained. There is, in fact, such a passionless quality to Nichols' portrayal of sexual behavior that at the close of the picture it comes as a shock to recall that Nichols deliberately avoids any portrayal of pleasure. It is its complete lack of eroticism that makes this tale of sexual preoccupation so dismal. There are moments of humor at the outset, especially in Arthur Garfunkel's fumbling attempts to meet Candice Bergen, but the film's overall tone is one of unrelieved pessimism. Such a mood suggests a vision of hopelessness, which is why this is no "entertainment" film, but rather a work of film art that requires careful consideration.

(September 2, 1971)

INDEX

133

135